# COLORADO IS CALLING

*Adventures in the Rocky Mountain State*

VIVA PURPOSE TRAVEL GUIDE BOOKS

## NIKKI PAGE

Book Cover Art: Viva Purpose, Inc.

Illustrations by Steve Page

Editor: Morgan Mosher

Photography by Nikki Page, Jered Bridgeman, Steve Page, and Taya Page

2 edition 2024 Printed in multiple countries worldwide

Library of Congress Control Number: 2024906216

ISBN-13 (E-book): 978-1-958716-10-6

ISBN-13 (Paperback): 978-1-958716-11-3

ISBN-13 (Hardcover): 978-1-958716-12-0

*To my parents, my constant source of guidance and inspiration. Your deep love for Colorado has instilled in me a profound appreciation for its stunning landscapes. The delightful moments we spent enjoying sweet cherry drinks, the thrilling hikes through the majestic Rockies, the laughter shared on vibrant Ferris wheels, and the adrenaline rush of standing on the world's highest bridge have all revealed the incredible diversity of this state. Your steadfast support has been the cornerstone of my journey, and I am eternally thankful.*

# CONTENTS

# ACKNOWLEDGMENTS

I want to start by expressing my gratitude to *Viva Purpose, Inc.* for giving me the opportunity to work on this incredible project. It has been a fantastic experience, and I am thankful for your trust in me.

My travel buddies, Chuck and Michele, thank you for hitting the trails with me. Taya Page at *Peculiar Pieces*, and Jered *BridgemanPhotography*, you two truly capture the beauty of Colorado through your lenses.

I want to extend a special thank you to Morgan Mosher at *Peculiar Pieces*. From editing to layout and design, the project was not easy, but you did an incredible job. Jan, thank you for speeding up the process. Kiki, you are an amazing assistant who shows up around the clock for me, and I am grateful for your dedication.

Colleen, thanks for sharing the views from the top of the Incline. Wendy and Amanda, you may not know this, but you two helped inspire me to write. Thanks for being my friends for decades. To all my teachers around the world, thank you for helping me learn and grow.

To my parents and in-laws, who have all been a part of this crazy adventure, and to my husband, Steve, and my four children, thank you for traveling this beautiful globe with me. Although you are grown now, I will always cherish the memories of watching you experience this wonderful world through fresh eyes.

I also want to express my heartfelt gratitude to the *National Parks, Forest Services*, and their dedicated workers. Your tireless efforts in preserving and maintaining these natural wonders are truly appreciated. A big thank you to all the places that offer free or affordable tours—your commitment to making Colorado's beauty accessible to everyone helps keep the state's tourism thriving.

To all my readers and fans, it has been an absolute pleasure traveling with you over the years. Thank you for your support and for joining me on this incredible journey.

# INTRODUCTION

Welcome to a journey through the heart of Colorado, a place that has captured my spirit and inspired this very guide. I am Nikki Page, and I've spent years immersing myself in the grandeur of my home state, from the silent majesty of the Rockies to the vibrant streets of our bustling cities. This book is the culmination of that adventure—an invitation to experience Colorado through the eyes of a native who has trekked its trails, savored its secrets, and delighted in its culinary treasures.

Inside these pages, you'll find a treasure trove of the Rockies' hidden gems and a sampling of the state's rich and diverse food scene, making it a dream for culinary enthusiasts. Alongside personal anecdotes and tips, this guide reveals the best spots to enjoy local flavors that complement the scenic backdrop. And yes, even a few bucket list items beckon me still, calling for future explorations.

As you hold this guide, know that it's more than a collection of destinations; it's a passport to the wonders of a state that continues to enchant and surprise, both with its natural beauty and its gastronomic delights.

Whether you're a seasoned traveler or setting foot in Colorado for the first time, I hope this book serves as your trusted companion on a journey that's as grand as the mountains themselves.

Let's discover together why this place has held me in its embrace for so long. Welcome to Colorado—let the adventure begin.

# CHAPTER 1

# EXPLORING THE HEART OF THE CENTENNIAL STATE

## COLORADO'S RICH TAPESTRY OF ADVENTURE AND BEAUTY

This western central state was founded in 1876, where a treasure trove of experiences awaits you. From adrenaline-pumping outdoor adventures to a sports enthusiast's paradise, the majestic Rocky Mountains provide the perfect backdrop for a holiday filled with unforgettable moments.

Whether you're drawn to exploring places indoors or venturing into the great outdoors, there's something here that will capture every heart.

Embark on a journey through Colorado's diverse offerings. Savor the local flavors, from expertly brewed beers and vibrant art scenes to sweet confections and thrilling outdoor escapades—this state truly has it all.

Discover the natural heritage, from the iconic state fossil, the Stegosaurus, to the towering Blue Spruce trees. Admire the delicate beauty of the Columbine flowers that dot the landscape or spot the Lark Bunting bird fluttering by. In Colorado, every visit is a voyage through nature's wonders and human ingenuity.

## Things to Keep in Mind
## When Traveling to the Western State

**Water is your friend**. It's essential to stay hydrated, particularly at high altitudes. Remember, Colorado is known as the Mile High State.

**Changing weather:** Dress in layers, because, as any Coloradan will tell you, if you don't like the weather, wait 10 minutes—it's bound to change! Depending on where you are in the state, you can experience a variety of weather conditions.

Expect large snowfalls, mild springs, and falls, as well as dry, hot summers in Colorado with low humidity, making the temperatures feel more tolerable, whether hot or cold. In the east, you might encounter tornadoes. The weather is so unpredictable that I was wearing shorts in March yesterday when it was a pleasant 75 degrees, but it snowed later that night. On other occasions, I have started my day in a sweater and long pants and ended the day in a tank top and shorts. This is especially true for the mountain areas. Layers are essential, that's all I can say.

**Preserving the Natural Tranquility**. Please respect our beautiful Colorado trails by staying on designated hiking paths and using ATVs only in marked areas. Ensure you have a license for fishing and hunting, and always stay within designated zones. Please stick to the trails as much as possible when hiking; this helps preserve our wildlife and vegetation.

**Pack it in, you pack it out!** It's unfortunate that this needs to be said, but it's an important reminder: PICK UP YOUR TRASH! As a hiker, I'm appalled at how often I see litter along these pristine paths. Our aim should always be to hike out with more trash than we brought in, helping to keep our forests clean and pristine for everyone to enjoy.

 *Now let's get to traveling the colorful state.*

# CHAPTER 2

# DENVER INTERNATIONAL AIRPORT: DIA

## WHAT'S REALLY GOING ON

**D**enver International Airport (DIA) is steeped in history. I remember watching the airport being built over a period of five years. It opened back in 1995, a year and a half behind schedule, due to numerous hold-ups, but the most memorable one was the baggage system that kept losing luggage. The total cost exceeded $4.8 billion. In today's dollars, that's around $8.5 billion, with $2.8 billion incurred during the months when the airport should have already been completed but was instead plagued by "problems." To this day, DIA remains the largest airport in North America and the second largest in the world.[1]

It replaced the smaller *Stapleton Airport*, transforming Denver into an international hub. The tent-like roof is a work of art in itself, designed by *Curt Fentress* and *James Bradburn* to represent the snow-capped Rocky Mountains.

A tribute to the wild west greets you in the form of a blue Mustang with fiery red eyes as it watches each car enter and exit the airport. Something you may not know about the sculpture **Blucifer** is that the artist, *Luis Jiménez*, tragically died when a part of the artwork fell on him in his studio. My dad would tell me the stories when we traveled, about how the horse was haunted and its eyes were watching us, reminding us not to bring anything illegal in and out of the airport because the horse's eyes have X-ray vision and could see through the cars. Now, I don't know if the X-ray part is a fact, but I do know that this piece of artwork is just one of the things that makes Denver unique.

There are many conspiracy theories surrounding this airport. When I was younger, I wasn't a big believer in conspiracy theories. However, thanks to a couple of my adult children and the state of the world over the years, I've somewhat opened my mind. If you're looking for a piece of artwork that makes you think a little more about what a *"New World"* looks like, this international hub is just the place. It's part of the new order, even marked in stone with the inscription, *"New World Airport Commission"*. [2]

When traveling through this airport, I encourage you to check out the east and west wings near baggage claim. After passing security, take a wander through each concourse and observe the artwork murals, which depict everything from starvation to pollution, death, and wars. The artist *Leo Tanguma* says the pieces were meant to depict world peace, but many, like myself, see the destitution and the fallout of the world.

Some speculate that there is a world hidden beneath the railway station that was built during the airport's massive construction project. I'm not sure what's under the airport rail system, but one thing is for sure, *Denver International Airport* is full of spectacular things to see. The views of the Rocky Mountains will leave you breathless as you arrive and depart.

As you touch down at *Denver International Airport (DIA)*, situated a mere 25 miles from the heart of the city, you're seamlessly connected to the downtown buzz via the **RTD train** on the "**A Line**". This efficient rail service, with frequent departures, is your stress-free gateway to the urban excitement that awaits. The train was easy and affordable costing us around $10 each way.

You can also save money by parking in off-site lots and taking a shuttle to the airport. One of my favorite strategies is to park at an airport hotel. Be sure to read reviews and assess the security, as each hotel offers varying levels of security. There are all kinds of chains that offer free parking if you book a night. There's nothing like being able to get a good night's sleep, shaving a couple of hours off the travel clock, and enjoying a free breakfast, then being dropped off right at your terminal.

Remember to leave extra time to get to the airport when pursuing one of these options, as a shuttle makes multiple stops. Our last trip took almost 45 minutes, although, it was better than paying an additional $200 for parking. It's also best to ask the hotel how to contact the shuttle service when you return and make sure to double-check that their buses run 24 hours a day to avoid any surprises.

# CHAPTER 3

# THE MILE HIGH CITY - DENVER

## EXPLORING THE HEART OF COLORADO

S et the stage for your Colorado escapade in Denver, the vibrant heart and capital of the state. This metropolis invites you to delve into its eclectic neighborhoods, immerse yourself in the arts at the Denver Art Museum, and savor the flavors of its booming culinary landscape. Discover the ultimate concert venues, notably the iconic **Red Rocks Amphitheater**, and find tranquility in the city's lush green spaces.[1]

Downtown Denver is a treasure trove for weekend explorers, harmoniously fusing city allure with the magnificence of nature. The Mile High City stands proud with its rich tapestry of history, pulsating arts and culture, exquisite dining, and endless outdoor pursuits. No matter your passion—be it art, gastronomy, or adventure—you'll find your niche here amidst historic landmarks, museums, eateries, and recreational spots.

So, come along—pack your spirit of discovery and set off for a weekend filled with the charm and adventure that only Denver, cradled in the arms of the Rockies, can provide. Perched at one mile above sea level, earning its moniker as the **Mile High City**, this presents a unique setting for a weekend escape that blends outdoor thrills with cultural richness.

Bask in Denver's generous sunshine, with over 300 sunny days a year, providing the ideal backdrop for a plethora of activities. Whether you're looking to hike the picturesque trails, cycle along scenic routes, or simply enjoy a picnic in one of the many parks, Denver's clear skies are your ally.

## Where to Stay in Denver
## Accommodations

If you're not sure where to stay during your visit, you can never go wrong with a location Downtown or in the adjacent **Lower Downtown (LoDo)** neighborhood. These areas offer easy access to premier attractions, dining, and entertainment options.

When planning a getaway to Denver, it's essential to select the perfect accommodations for your stay.

There are many choices for hotels in Downtown Denver.

Located in the historic Denver Union Station, **The Crawford Hotel** offers an elegant experience with easy access to a range of restaurants and shops.[2]

Part of *Marriott's Autograph Collection,* this iconic landmark, **The**

**Brown Palace Hotel and Spa** has been providing luxury accommodations since 1892. The exquisite architecture and top-notch service make it a favorite choice for travelers.

For a unique and personalized experience, consider a *boutique hotel* like **The Maven Hotel at Dairy Block**. Located in the Dairy Block, *The Maven* is in the heart of downtown and offers an eclectic mix of modern furnishings and local art.

Our accommodation choice was the **Embassy Suites** in downtown Denver, perfectly situated in the pulsing center of the city. The hotel offered us a generously sized and inviting room, complete with a cozy king-size bed, a living room area with a sofa, and a substantial desk space plus a table for added convenience. The room's modern decor created a soothing atmosphere, ideal for unwinding after a day of exploration.

One of the highlights of our room at the *Embassy Suites* was the mini kitchenette. It provided the convenience of preparing our snacks and brewing fresh coffee, adding a touch of home comfort to our Denver visit. This amenity was particularly appreciated, as it allowed us to enjoy light meals and warm beverages at our leisure, making our stay even more enjoyable. Step outside and you're surrounded by great restaurants, shops, and things to do. It's the perfect home base for exploring all that Denver has to offer. With nice rooms at a very convenient downtown location. I highly recommend the *Embassy Suites* if you're visiting Denver.[3]

Once you've chosen your accommodation, it's time to explore the diverse attractions of Downtown Denver. The city offers a variety of transportation options to make getting around a breeze.

Even if you're staying in a hotel in downtown Denver, be ready for higher-than-average parking prices. Hotel parking garages typically charge $50-$80 per night. Street parking meters start at $1-2 per hour, that's if you can even find one. We paid $52 per night at our hotel and that was before the valet tip.

If you plan to drive and park in downtown Denver, factor parking costs into your budget. The good news is Denver has an excellent public transit system called *RTD*. Taking the train or bus lets you explore downtown without a car, saving you parking fees. Denver's transit also makes it easy to leave your car at the hotel and explore car-free.

## Exploring Downtown Denver

When visiting Downtown Denver, there are countless attractions and hotspots to fill your vacation. Experience the bustling 16th Street Mall, catch a home run in the **Rockpile** at **Coors Field**, or explore the historic sites; there's something for everyone in this thriving city center.

First on our itinerary is the iconic ***16th Street Mall***, stretching 1.25 miles through the heart of downtown. We marvel at the collection of shops, restaurants, and landmarks that line this pedestrian-friendly strip. Whether we're in the mood for fine dining or a quick bite, this lively area has it all. Public art and street performers add flair and energy to the atmosphere as we stroll along.

Venturing a few blocks west, we find ourselves in *LoDo*, the city's oldest neighborhood. Rich in history, *LoDo* offers us a glimpse of Denver's past with its preserved architectural landmarks and nineteenth-century structures. It's here that we discover *Larimer Square*, the birthplace of Denver, where the first buildings were established. Today, *Larimer Square h*as evolved into a hub of trendy shops, boutiques, restaurants, and vibrant nightlife.

Getting around, as we explore Denver's thriving community, we can't help but appreciate the ease of navigating the cityscape. The city offers bike-sharing options, making it a breeze to access all these amenities.

Discovering Denver's charm can be both unique and eco-friendly by taking advantage of the ***Denver B-cycle***, the city's affordable bike-sharing program with convenient stations peppered throughout the city. Glide through the heart of Downtown Denver at your leisure, uncovering an array of hidden treasures along the way. This delightful mode of transportation not only allows you to soak in the urban sights but also supports a greener environment.

Scooters are another fun option to weave through the city streets, and they are often easier to find than bikes. Scooters are especially handy for travelers mindful of their budget. However, it's important to keep an eye on expenses, as service fees can accumulate with each new ride. Check the fee table in the app. We learned that these charges apply each time you hop on and off, so plan your trips wisely to get the most out of your sightseeing experience without unnecessary costs. These nifty forms of transportation can be found throughout the city; you can simply jump on and off the scooters or bikes at your destination.

## Top Sightseeing Spots

During our getaway to Downtown Denver, we visited several remarkable sightseeing spots that deserve a mention. First on our remarkable list is *Union Station,* a **historical landmark** that was once considered the oldest building in the West, originally opening in 1881 as a transportation hub.[4]

Beautifully restored in 1894 after a fire, this architectural gem now houses popular shops and restaurants, making it a bustling spot for both locals and tourists.

ARTS AND CULTURE

## Denver Art Museum

The city's vibrant and diverse culture sets it apart and ensures that there is something for everyone to enjoy. A must-visit for art enthusiasts is the *Denver Art Museum*.[5] With its impressive collection of contemporary, Native American, and Western art, this museum captivated our imagination and left us awe-inspired. The unique architecture of the building alone is worth seeing. These are just a few examples of the exceptional art and cultural experiences available.

During a recent visit to the *River North Art District (RiNo),* my youngest daughter and I spent hours meandering through the vibrant streets, captivated by the graffiti art that adorned the walls.[6] What some might simply pass by, we saw as a rich tapestry of urban creativity, a form of expression I've grown to deeply appreciate over the years.

This shared love for street art first came to light when we lived in Costa Rica and embarked on a girls' trip to the city of San Jose. It was there, amidst the colorful chaos, where my daughter's fascination became undeniable.

These experiences, both in Costa Rica and in the heart of Denver, have become cherished memories, bonding us over our mutual admiration for the raw and powerful voice of street art.

The **Denver Children's Museum** is a downtown treasure, offering interactive fun for kids from infancy to eight years old.[7] It's a place where young explorers can learn through play, whether they're climbing in the playground or discovering the wonders of a storybook-like world. Perfect for a family day out, the museum provides educational activities that captivate the imagination and encourage learning in a playful environment.

**The Bellco Theatre**, located within the convention center, is a venue for concerts, comedy shows, and other performances, providing both entertainment and educational opportunities to attendees.[8]

## Colorado History

Our next stop was the renowned ***Clyfford Still Museum***, a must-visit for art enthusiasts. The museum exclusively showcases the works of *Clyfford Still*, a leading figure in the Abstract Expressionism movement.[9] Through the museum's captivating exhibitions, we gained a deeper understanding of his unique approach to art and his significant impact on the art world.

We then made our way to the ***Kirkland Museum of Fine and Decorative Art***, which houses objects spanning over 150 years of artistic movement. [10] The museum's diverse collections offered a fascinating insight into the evolution of art, design, and creativity throughout history.

As history buffs, we couldn't miss the ***History Colorado Center***, a treasure trove of interactive exhibits that tell the story of Colorado's rich past. From the state's Indigenous roots to its thriving present, we found ourselves immersed in stories that shaped the land and its people.

While in the neighborhood, we visited the famous ***Molly Brown House Museum***.[11] This beautifully preserved Victorian home of the legendary Margaret "Molly Brown" – a philanthropist, socialite, and Titanic survivor – offers a unique glimpse into the life and times of a remarkable woman and her impact on Denver's history.

The highlight of our cultural experience in Downtown Denver was attending a performance at the ***Denver Center for the Performing Arts***.[12] Home to multiple venues featuring a variety of shows, from Broadway plays, to contemporary dance, and symphonic concerts, it's no wonder this iconic institution is a beloved destination for both locals and visitors alike.

An urban oasis with cultural highlights, another fascinating destination was the **Colorado State Capitol** building. Located in the heart of Denver, this stunning structure features a golden dome that shines bright in the Colorado capital city. Climb its 99 steps to enjoy the picturesque views of the mountains and the city skyline, and learn about Colorado's rich history during your visit. I also want to point out this is a *free guided tour*.

Situated near the *Colorado State Capitol*, the **Civic Center Park** is a place for cultural events, festivals, concerts, and more. Boasting Greek-inspired architecture, fountains, and flower gardens, *Civic Center Park* is an excellent spot for relaxation and admiring downtown Denver.[13]

*We found some cool rocking chairs outside that provided a perfect spot*
*to rest*
*our tired feet.*

**Denver City Park** is more than just a park; it's a cultural and recreational hub that offers something for everyone, whether you're looking to relax in nature, educate yourself and your family, or simply enjoy the beauty of the park as it lights up for the holidays. *Denver City Park* is an expansive green haven in the heart of the city, offering a relaxing setting for picnics, leisurely walks, and a multitude of recreational activities.

While in the area, immerse yourself in the wonders of wildlife at the **Denver Zoo**, which also dazzles visitors with its festive holiday lights display, transforming the zoo into a twinkling nocturnal wonderland during the season. After exploring the animal exhibits, you can engage with the mysteries of the cosmos or the intricacies of the natural world at the **Denver Museum of Nature & Science**. Don't miss the chance to enhance your visit with an awe-inspiring **IMAX** movie that brings breathtaking scenes from around the globe to a larger-than-life format.

## A Fusion of Culinary Delights and Craft Beer Mastery

In addition to the cultural attractions, Denver offers a wide range of culinary experiences and a thriving craft beer scene. From farm-to-table dining to award-winning breweries, the city continues to make its mark on the national food and beverage stage. During your getaway to Denver, a food and drink experience is an integral part of the journey. You can start the day off with a delicious breakfast at one of the many cafes and bakeries in the city. Denver offers a rich selection of restaurants, perfect for fueling your urban exploration.

As you venture further into Downtown, you will find a diverse range of culinary choices, including contemporary American cuisine and unique international offerings. One of our must-visit stops is the **Denver Milk Market**, a food hall featuring 16 individual vendors serving mouth-watering dishes. With options ranging from fresh seafood to Italian-style pizza, the *Milk Market* provides a unique and delightful dining experience for every palate.

Denver is renowned for its flourishing craft beer scene. Enthusiasts can embark on brewery tours, sampling some of the finest craft beers the country has to offer. With a multitude of breweries and bars in close proximity, it's effortless to hop from one tasting room to the next, uncovering a diverse array of exceptional brews along the way.

If cocktails are more your style, then you're in for a treat, as Downtown Denver boasts numerous bars serving up exquisite drinks. You can indulge in creative libations crafted by top-notch bartenders, each concoction offering dazzling flavors that are sure to elevate your spirits. Whether you prefer a hoppy IPA or a meticulously mixed cocktail, Denver's vibrant downtown has something to satisfy every palate.

As the day turns to night, the city doesn't slow down. The nightlife in Denver is as diverse as its daytime offerings, with rooftop bars, speakeasies, and dance clubs that cater to every taste. The city's craft beer culture is particularly noteworthy, with an impressive selection of microbreweries and taprooms offering tours and tastings.

Even my husband Steve Page, who is a seasoned travel author, was pleasantly surprised by the selection of whiskies at **Coyote Ugly Saloon** in downtown Denver. Squeezed between bustling bars along

*Larimer Square*, this casual watering hole doesn't look like much from the outside, just a couple of big bar bouncers guarding the door. But step inside and over 100 whiskies - including rare finds from Scotland, Ireland, and beyond - line the back shelf.

Steve enjoyed an *18-year-old Lagavulin single malt Scotch*. Whether you're a whisky aficionado or just looking to discover a new favorite dram, Coyote Ugly is worth adding to your Denver itinerary.

To compliment the fantastic drinks, there were some wild dance games happening. To the girl who danced on top of the table, you certainly earned those extra tips. It's been quite a while since I've seen someone move with such agility and rhythm, and I've never witnessed a man's face turn so red so quickly. Your confidence was off the charts, and while I'm still not sure I could ever partake in a public body shot like the one you allowed him to do, it was definitely a memorable spectacle for everyone there.

Another highlight for beer enthusiasts visiting Denver, is the **Denver Beer Trail**. This self-guided tour is an adventure through the city's bustling craft beer scene, with over 100 breweries to explore. It's an opportunity to delve into a wide array of beer styles, from the classic lagers and ales to more experimental and seasonal brews. Each brewery on the trail has its unique character and specialties, offering a taste of Denver's diverse beer culture. A tour of a brewery offers a diverse and engaging experience that extends beyond the simple enjoyment of beer.

Many breweries create a vibrant and welcoming atmosphere by incorporating indoor and outdoor areas with comfortable seating and a variety of games. These spaces provide an ideal setting for socializing and enjoying the brewery's offerings in a relaxed environment. Patrons can sit back with a freshly poured pint and engage in a friendly competition over games like *Cornhole*, giant *Jenga*, or *Skeetch* (a local favorite bar game that was created in Colorado), making for a memorable visit.

The *Denver Beer Trail* is not just about sipping on different beers; it's a chance to meet the brewers, hear their stories, and understand the community and collaboration that define Denver's beer scene. Whether you're a casual drinker or a connoisseur, the trail provides a chance to discover new favorites and appreciate the creativity and craftsmanship that go into every pour.

A brewery tour can offer an enriching experience that combines education, entertainment, and the pleasure of craft beer. When in Denver, the Beer Trail invites visitors to embark on a flavorful journey through the heart of the city's thriving beer culture, making it a must-do activity for anyone looking to experience the local vibe and the art of brewing.

About 20 minutes north-west of Denver, Arvada (another suburb) is home to **School House Kitchen and Libations**, which knocked it out of the park. As a cookbook author, I was delighted by their ingenious nachos, never having considered the clever use of a flour tortilla at the bottom to scoop up the delicious leftovers.

The plate was wiped clean amidst the charming ambiance of Arvada. Childhood nostalgia meets gourmet delights. This past Halloween, we embarked on an adventure that led us to this culinary gem, transporting us back to the whimsy of our childhoods. Dressed in festive costumes, we entered a world scented with old spice and adorned with vintage tables, a room that whispered of scholarly pursuits, complete with a wall of scotch that promised tales of its own.

The iconic **Big Blue Bear** sculpture is officially titled *I See What You Mean*. Created by artist *Lawrence Argent*, the 40-foot-tall blue bear peers curiously into the glass facade of the **Colorado Convention Center**, becoming a beloved symbol of the city and a popular photo opportunity for visitors and locals alike.[14]

## Something for Everyone

The *Colorado Convention Center* is a multipurpose venue that hosts a wide array of events throughout the year. These events range from trade shows and conventions to consumer shows and corporate events, including outdoor recreation shows like fishing and RV expos, auto shows, book fairs, and many others. Steve even remembers fishing in a big tank during a father-and-son outing when he was younger.

The *Colorado Convention Center* is known for its sizable exhibit halls, state-of-the-art facilities, and the charm it brings to downtown Denver. Denver is not only known for its tourism but also for its thriving business hub.

If exploring an underwater world captivates your interest, then the **Denver Aquarium** is an attraction I highly recommend. Over the years, I've visited this expansive aquatic haven several times, and quite often when my children were younger. It's conveniently located right in the heart of downtown, making it an accessible escape into the wonders of marine life. Each visit brings its own unique discoveries and delights, from the mesmerizing dance of the jellyfish to the playful antics of the otters.

The *Denver Aquarium* is not just a place to see marine creatures— it's an educational journey that has provided countless memories for my family. With a 500-species panoramic view of their 400,000-gallon Shipwreck exhibit, you can encounter Sand Tiger sharks, Sandbar sharks, Zebra sharks, Blacktip sharks, Bamboo sharks, and hundreds of other fish. Beyond the aquatic, you might even catch a glimpse of mermaids gliding gracefully or witness the majesty of a tiger, adding a touch of the surreal to your visit. The experiences here promise to capture your heart and create memories to cherish.

If your sense of wonder tempts you to explore the unexpected, Denver's **Meow Wolf** is a destination that's been whispered about with enthusiasm, particularly by my son who has ventured there multiple times.

This interactive art experience defies easy description, promising a journey through realms of the fantastical and whimsical. Though I have yet to step into this imaginative odyssey, its reputation precedes it, painting vivid tales of a sensory-rich adventure.

*Meow Wolf* remains high on my list of must-visit places, and I eagerly anticipate the day I can immerse myself in its extraordinary narrative tapestry.

***Hammonds Candy*** offers a factory tour and is one of my favorite free tours in Colorado. I still remember the first time we took this tour. Despite all my years in Colorado, I had never seen candy canes being made. I've seen caramels and fudges in Estes Park, Colorado Springs, Manitou, and even downtown Fort Collins. It was the perfect outing for the kids. Watching colorful molten sugar being stretched on the old-time machines for aeration and crafted by hand was educational. I think my eyes were just as wide as my kids' as we watched all the different kinds of candy being prepared. The gift shop at the end was just as delightful; we enjoyed the free samples and stocked up on various flavors of sweet treats. Keep in mind that you're in a candy factory—stay away if you are sick. As of my last update, this factory still requires masks, and be aware that the facility is closed on Sundays.

Not far from downtown Denver, **Top Golf** is right off I-25 in the town of Thornton and it's worth the short trip. To make the most of your visit, I recommend booking online or calling ahead to reserve a spot on the top tier. The top floor is best, especially at night.

The view from up there is killer, offering a stunning backdrop to your game. It's a fantastic way to spend an evening, engaging in what I would describe as a hybrid of virtual and real-life golf.

The unique blend of technology and physical sport creates an experience that's both innovative and enjoyable, perfect for golf enthusiasts and newcomers alike. Whether you're there for the sport, the atmosphere, or the view, *Top Golf* is a standout destination for an entertaining night out. The facility has a couple of bars, and the food was also a hit.

*Tip:*
*They have heaters, but we still needed our hats and jackets on our first visit because our trip was in late December.*

Of course, we cannot overlook the city's passion for professional sports. With top-tier teams like the **Denver Broncos (NFL)**, **Colorado Rockies (MLB)**, **Denver Nuggets (NBA)**, *and* **Colorado Avalanche (NHL)** there's always a thrilling game to catch at one of the many stadiums and coliseums in the downtown arena.

Let's make some money. The **Denver Mint** might be a place where money is made, but the tour is free. It's one of only four locations in the US where you can witness currency being produced. The only downside is no babies or little ones are allowed, you must be 7 years or older to take the educational tour. Additionally, tickets are available on a first-come, first-served basis, so be sure to arrive early to secure your spot.

The **Denver Butterfly Pavilion** is an amazing place to witness a kaleidoscope of incredible butterflies, boasting a population of over 1,500 fluttering wonders.

It offers much more than just a visual spectacle; this was the first place my son had the unforgettable experience of holding Rosie the Tarantula, who is about ready to celebrate her 29th birthday—remarkably, as old as the Pavilion itself.

The Pavilion provides an exceptional setting for hands-on learning and immersive experiences, such as taking a leisurely stroll through the tropical gardens to admire the vibrant butterflies.

In addition to the local inhabitants, visitors can explore the Costa Rica exhibit, which transports you to the lush rainforests and rich biodiversity of Central America. The Butterfly Pavilion is a place where the beauty of nature is within arm's reach and every visit promises a new discovery.

Embark on a nostalgic trip to the **Denver National Western Stock Show**, the pinnacle event that has been upholding Colorado's Western heritage as the largest stock show since its inception in 1906. For those who've never witnessed the spectacle of a stock show, it's an essential experience that brings together a variety of animals, top-tier cattle, dynamic auctions, and the dedicated youth of 4H clubs with their hard-won ribbons.

The stock show's rich history began under the grand expanse of what was once the largest circus tent in the world. Today, it has evolved into a state-of-the-art complex, continuing the tradition of educating and entertaining with a nod to the Wild West. Attendees can immerse themselves in the excitement of a rodeo, marvel at the precision of horseback riders, and savor a culinary experience that harkens back to childhood delights. The aromas of cotton candy, the vibrant spectacle of snow cones, and the classic flavor of roasted peanuts are just a few of the treats that evoke fond childhood memories and celebrate the enduring spirit of the West.

Did you forget your cowboy attire? Don't worry, they have you covered. Step into the world of Western fashion with a wide selection of boots and observe skilled artisans as they customize cowboy hats to your liking. Explore the craftsmanship of leatherwork and browse through an array of silver and gold jewelry. Whether you're looking to complete your Western wardrobe or seeking a unique souvenir, you'll find everything you need to embrace the cowboy spirit. The *Denver National Western Stock Show* is not just an event; it's a journey through the past and present of Colorado's Western identity.

### *Fun Rides and Fast Roller Coasters*

*Elitch Gardens*, once celebrated for its lush gardens, movie theaters, and ballroom, has been a beloved destination for generations. Many families, like mine, have fond memories of summer trips to this enchanting botanic park.

Known for its whimsical gardens and thrilling rides, including the infamous wooden roller coaster *Twister, Elitch Gardens* has been a cornerstone of Denver's entertainment history.

Originally family-owned and operated, the park underwent significant changes after its relocation to downtown Denver in 1993. The cost was somewhere around $95 million to move the park, bringing with it new thrill rides and a water park to enhance the experience and gain more of a modern downtown feel but losing the botanical garden feeling. It was eventually bought out and incorporated into the *Six Flags* name in 1998, then it dropped *Six Flags* off in 2007 when the park changed owners again. Over 131 years of creating memories and history in Denver, there's a bittersweet announcement that the park will be demolished. However, the spirit of *Elitch Gardens Theme & Water Park* will continue, much like it did in 1993, with plans to rebuild with more space—this time potentially in Aurora. The legacy of *Elitch Gardens* as a place of joy and amusement is set to carry on for future generations to enjoy.

A nostalgic journey that steps back in time is a visit to **Lakeside Amusement Park**. It is Colorado's oldest amusement park and is located in Lakewood. The park has been family-owned since 1908.

Known as **The White City of the West** for its twinkling lights, this historic gem is the last of the *White Cities* to remain operational after many others closed during the Depression.[15] It boasts the *Tower of Jewels*, an impressive 150-foot structure that once held the title of the tallest building in Colorado.

While the park has evolved, prohibiting activities like swimming in the lake and gambling, it continues to thrill visitors with rides like the *Ferris Wheel, Chipmunk Roller Coaster,* and the *Rock-O-Plane*.

Admission is convenient with free parking and a choice of a small entrance fee with individual ride tickets. For those planning to enjoy numerous rides, the wristband offers great value for unlimited fun. Remember to check the park's hours and days of operation, as it typically closes during the week on Tuesday. [16]

❦

My first encounter with **Casa Bonita,** a childhood gem, was as a six-year-old when its doors swung open in 1980. It often marked the grand finale of a fun-filled day at *Lakeside Amusement Park* or was the destination for a special family outing.[17]

The distinctive big pink building, complete with a water fountain, holds a dear place in my memories. It was there that my sister and I would toss our pennies and make wishes before joining the queue to collect our trays and make our way through the cafeteria line offering Mexican food.

While the cuisine at *Casa Bonita* was not particularly renowned, it was the entertainment that truly made the experience unforgettable. The spectacle of cliff divers plunging from lofty heights beside a waterfall, the exploration of a cave, and the mystery of a dragon's mouth captivated us as we dined.

*Casa Bonita* was designated a city **historical landmark** in 2015 but faced a temporary closure in 2021 due to the pandemic, followed by a bankruptcy filing.[18] In a twist of fate, the iconic eatery was purchased by the creators of *South Park* who reimagined the restaurant's possibilities.[19] I have yet to enjoy the newly remodeled dining experience, but I eagerly anticipate the day I do. I have been told the new owners have infused the beloved establishment with fresh energy while preserving its essence. They've brought in a new chef and continue to offer the cherished unlimited sopapillas, alongside the classic water features and diving performances.

A gateway to unforgettable experiences and cherished memories, Denver is not only a fantastic destination for the attractions within the city, but it also serves as a great starting point for exploring the natural beauty and history of Colorado. The city's proximity to the Rocky Mountains allows for easy day trips to iconic spots like *Rocky Mountain National Park, Pikes Peak*, and *Red Rocks Amphitheater*. With its diverse blend of art, culture, and history, Downtown Denver truly offers a memorable escape to satisfy any traveler, and we enjoyed every moment of our enriching experience.

The city's elevation isn't just a point of pride—it's an invitation to adventure seekers. The nearby Rocky Mountains beckon with their snow-capped peaks and clear, blue skies, offering a natural playground for skiing, snowboarding, and mountain climbing. For those who prefer a more relaxed pace, the city's numerous green spaces and botanical gardens offer a peaceful respite from the urban energy. It is easy to see why Denver should be at the top of your list for your next getaway. With its sun-soaked adventures, rich culture, and mountainous backdrop, the "Mile High City" is sure to leave you with unforgettable experiences and memories.

Another common area of interest is the ***Denver Tech Center***, just

26 miles from *Denver International Airport (DIA)*. The *DTC* is in *Greenwood Village*, a suburb of Denver. In addition to conventions, the center is equipped to host lectures, seminars, and meetings, offering a variety of spaces such as ballrooms and meeting rooms of different sizes. Many hotels offer a complimentary drink and appetizer around the 5 o'clock hour. If you're not renting a car, the best way to reach the *Tech Center* is by *RTD* bus or rideshare. I'm sure a train service will be available someday, but for now, the bus or rideshare are your go-to options.

Do you enjoy dressing up in elaborate attire? If so, you'll be delighted by Larkspur, Colorado. Not quite an hour south of *Denver International Airport (DIA)* and close to the *Denver Tech Center,* and Castle Rock; Larkspur is renowned for its annual **Renaissance Festival**, which takes place from June to August. This festive gathering celebrates not only the historical pageantry of medieval times, but also the end of winter and the joy of rebirth. Imagine a world of jousting, feasting, and dancing—a perfect celebration of renewal and tradition. The festival is a showcase for some of the most amazing handmade costumes inspired by medieval times.

CHAPTER 4

# EASTERN PLAINS BACK
# IN TIME

## A JOURNEY THROUGH PREHISTORIC
## WONDERS AND HIDDEN HISTORIES

Although most tourist activity is located west of I-25, which runs north and south through Colorado dividing the mountainous regions from the Great Plains, there are a few spots worth mentioning in the east. If you only have a short time in Colorado these are probably not top priorities but if you are on a road trip coming from the east they are worth checking out.

If you find yourself on the eastern plains of Colorado, make sure to stop by the **Kit Carson County Fairgrounds** in **Burlington**, where you can see the original carousel from the *Elitch Gardens Amusement Park* in Denver. Located around two and half hours east of DIA near the Colorado-Kansas border you can witness this piece of history. As one of the oldest carousels in the country, you can appreciate the hand-carved and painted animals and carts as well as the decorative structure of the carousel. The craftsmanship of the *Philadelphia Toboggan Company Carousel #6* is not only impressive but is a representation of the history of woodcarving.[1]

Embark on a journey to the **Paint Mines Interpretive Park**, an awe-inspiring natural landmark listed on the U.S. National Register of Historic Places.[2,3] Located less than 2 hours southeast of DIA near the town of **Calhan**, the **Badlands** within the park are a sight to behold, with their array of soft pastel colors drawing the eye.

Spanning 750 acres, the *Paint Mines Archaeological District* is a testament to the beauty of the natural world. According to legend, the spires were painted with clay pigments by Native Americans more than 9,000 years ago, adding a layer of historical mystique to the vibrant formations.

Continuing south and east we go further back in time. A two-hour drive from Calhan, or a direct 3 hours from DIA, is the small town of **La Junta**. To the south, the rugged canyons nestled within the **Comanche National Grasslands** serve as the backdrop for *North* America's most extensive *dinosaur track site,* **Picketwire Canyon Trackway**.[4] Here, more than 1,900 footprints create 130 distinct pathways, sprawling over a quarter-mile stretch of bedrock adjacent to the **Purgatoire River's** shoreline. Most of the tracks at this site belong to *Apatosaurus* or *Allosaurus*, with the former's prints indicating herding behavior and the latter's showing signs of a predatory chase, including evidence of group hunting strategies. An intriguing section known as the "trample zone" features overlapping footprints and distinct tail drag marks, which point to the mating behavior of Apatosaurus with their rigid, upright tails. If you are a dinosaur buff it's a must-see.

Even the spiders love Colorado. Thousands of Oklahoma brown tarantulas migrate through the state looking for their mates. From September to October, you can watch this happen with your own eyes. Many may find it unusual; however, Colorado celebrates this *La Junta Tarantula Festival* every year.[5] Food trucks, face painting, parades, and even watching the eight-legged creatures search for their mates are all part of the festivities.

You can even view the *Largest Self-Supported Log Roof in the World*, a registered state historic site by the Colorado Historical Society.[6] The *Koshare Museum*, built by the Boy Scout troop under the inspired leadership of James Francis "Buck" Burshears, houses a world-class collection of Native American art and artifacts, considered to be among the finest globally.

The inspiration for this remarkable structure came during the Koshares' trips to Aztec National Monument in 1939, 1941, and 1946. While there, the boys listened intently to the ranger's stories about the prehistoric Indians who built the great ceremonial Kivas a thousand years ago. Moved by these ancient tales, the Koshares decided to invest their surplus money in constructing a giant Kiva of their own.

The original 1949 structure, now a registered state historic site, stands as a testament to the Koshares' dedication and fascination with Native American culture. The museum's collection showcases the rich heritage and artistry of various Native American tribes, offering visitors a unique opportunity to explore and appreciate these ancient civilizations.

Even if you have seen Indian dancers before, watching the performances by the *Koshare Dancers*, a group of talented people, is a must and an enlightening experience.[7] The Koshare Dancers are members of Boy Scout Troop 232 and Venturing Crew 2230 of the Rocky Mountain Council, Boy Scouts of America. Another inexpensive activity is visiting the museum, with admission around $5, depending on your age, and children six and under admitted for free.

Decades of growing up in Colorado, and I never knew about all the things that could be done on the eastern plains and in the little town of La Junta. There will be no tarantulas for me; however, I'm looking forward to painting rocks and discovering dinosaur fossils, and maybe even making a stop to see the old carousel that I once rode in my younger years.

# CHAPTER 5

# COLORADO SPRINGS

## INDULGING IN LUXURY, NATURE, AND COSMIC WONDERS

S ituated 70 miles south of Denver and at an elevation of 6,035 feet, **Colorado Springs** offers breathtaking views (pun intended), including the majestic **Pikes Peak** mountain. Alternatively, you can fly into *Colorado Springs Municipal Airport (COS)*. [1]

The city, founded in 1871 by General William Jackson Palmer, a Civil War hero and railroad industry leader, showcases the enduring legacy of its founder, from the city streets to the mountain's summit.

American explorer Zebulon Pike named the peak *Highest Peak* in 1806, and it stands taller than any point in the United States east of its longitude. The towering peaks welcome visitors even before they enter the city, hinting at the natural grandeur that awaits.

As you head in on Highway 125 from Denver, you can spot a large aircraft and stadium—it's the ***United States Air Force Academy***.[2]

Protected from above and below the earth's surface, Colorado Springs hosts a handful of military facilities. Over the years, two have stood out to me because they left their mark. If you're lucky, you might even see the ***U.S. Navy*** or ***Thunderbirds*** jets flying high and fast in the sky.

Many parts of the academy are open to the public, where you can see aircraft displays up close, read about the rich history of the *Air Force*, take in the spectacular views, and even hike trails throughout the campus. All you have to do is show a *photo ID* at the gate and answer a couple of questions. The guard also asks to pop the car trunk to take a look inside. Additional restrictions apply to non-residents. Check the Academy website for specifics.

This particular outing had been on my bucket list for a long time. I had never even considered all the activities that would be free to do. First, you can visit the ***Visitor Center***, where you can take a *free tour* to learn about the history of the U.S. Air Force and the campus. There's also a viewing center where you can watch a short film about cadet life.

The historical ***United States Air Force Cadet Chapel,*** completed in 1962 and standing at a proud 150 feet, is an all-faith sanctuary that required $3.5 million for the construction of the building's shell and surrounding grounds. It won the *Twenty-five Year Award* from the American Institute of Architects in 1996, an accolade given to buildings that have "stood the test of time" for a period of 25-35 years. The chapel became a historical landmark in 2004.[3,4] Its organ along with various artifacts, and gifts from many different organizations, contribute to its rich tapestry of history and community contributions.

The chapel is famous for its 17-spired roof, which was originally planned to have twenty-one spires but was reduced due to budget constraints. The rain gutters were also omitted from the final plan. On our recent visit, it was disheartening to see large walls of barriers surrounding the iconic spires and that we were unable to tour the inside either. The chapel closed in 2019 for restoration due to water damage. Our guide mentioned that there were more "Home Depot buckets" than people in the pews when it rained.

The landmark was supposed to reopen in 2023. Instead, construction walls that had been erected still stand after asbestos was discovered, causing restoration costs to skyrocket. These costs are now expected to reach $220 million, with a projected completion date of 2027. You guessed it—this site has been added back to my bucket list as a place to experience once renovations are completed.

Watch the planes and gliders take off and land at the ***USAF Academy Airfield***. Colorado is known for training some of the best pilots in the world, and they must master the skill of landing without engines. I've always marveled at the ability to fly an aircraft like this. A small glider with no engine is attached by a tether to an aircraft with an engine. It's taken high into the air, where the other pilot will release the cable, allowing the glider to descend gracefully, with the pilot trying to catch the updrafts to perform loops in the sky. The runway was right in front of us as we watched these gliders takeoff and land.

I'm sure it's as scary as all get-out, but what I would give to feel the freedom of flying through the air like that. Sorry, I didn't get pictures of the takeoff; I was like a kid at an airshow, jumping up and down with each takeoff and landing. Next time, I'll bring a packed lunch and spend the day watching the runway.

In the same parking lot, you can see the *F-16 Fighting Falcon*, from the prestigious *USAF Thunderbirds*, and a picturesque view of *Pikes Peak* in the background. If you look closely at the very top of the picture, you can see a white speck. That speck is a plane towing a glider. The parking lot and benches were empty making the airshow feel like a private viewing. A round of applause to the amazing pilots—I was the enthusiastic spectator cheering you on as you made your landing.

Turning around provides the perfect photo opportunity with the *A-10 Thunderbolt II ground attack aircraft*. You can also see a *B-52 Stratofortress strategic bomber* and a *T-38 Talon jet trainer*.

The **U.S. Air Force Academy Planetarium**, originally built in 1959, is one of the oldest structures on the campus. After closing in 2004 due to outdated technology, it remained vacant for over 15 years. However, it reopened in 2019, thanks to the support of private donors who funded the reconstruction and a 360-degree near-hemispheric screen.

This development was a delightful surprise and not at all how we expected to spend our day. I am immensely grateful to all the private donors who made the renovation possible. Steve and I spent an entire afternoon immersed in free **IMAX** films, a treat that was both educational and entertaining.

Another marvel is **Cheyenne Mountain**, which can be seen from almost every point in Colorado Springs. This impressive peak is more than just a natural wonder shaped by Mother Nature; it's an integral part of our rich history, housing one of our nation's most vital military communication centers. Deep within the Colorado mountains of El Paso County lies the *Cheyenne Mountain Complex*, originally home to *NORAD*, the *North American Aerospace Defense Command*.[5] This facility was the epicenter of vigilance during the Cold War, with *NORAD* monitoring the skies for global aerial threats.

Constructed with the assistance of the Navy and the expertise of gold miners, the complex was a bulwark of American defense. While the main command center has since been moved to **Peterson Schriever Space Force Base**, previously *Peterson Air Force Base* 15-miles away, the legacy of *Cheyenne Mountain* endures.[6] The complex still boasts an underground town, complete with everything from gyms to lakes—some even equipped with boats—and a reservoir of diesel fuel to ensure backup power for generators.

The *Cheyenne Mountain Complex* stands as a testament to military ingenuity and preparedness, demonstrating that strategic use of our landscape goes beyond reaching mountain summits; it also involves the strategic occupation of their inner depths.

⚜

The ***Olympic and Paralympic Training Center*** in Colorado Springs stands as a testament to Colorado's profound commitment to the *Olympic and Paralympic* movements.[7] This world-class facility not only provides a high-altitude training environment that enhances athletes' endurance but also serves as a home away from home for up to 512 athletes aspiring to reach the pinnacle of their respective sports.

The center's roots are intertwined with the history of the *Paralympic Games*, which began with the Stoke Mandeville Games in 1948. These games were created to aid the rehabilitation of World War II veterans who, due to their injuries, became wheelchair-bound. This initiative set the stage for the *Paralympic Games*, a celebration of the athleticism and competitive spirits of athletes with disabilities that continues to inspire people around the world.

Visitors to the *Olympic and Paralympic Training Center* can explore the Visitor Center at no cost, where they can immerse themselves in the history of the Olympics, including the thrill of sitting in a bobsled.

Adjacent to the bobsled is the media room where many of the world's most elite athletes have been interviewed. Don't forget to check out the gift shop and get your *Team USA* gear. The grounds also feature a sculpture garden, which adds a touch of tranquility to this inspiring experience.

For those eager to understand the level of commitment required to compete at the highest levels, the center offers affordable tours that reveal the extensive support systems designed to assist both *Olympic and Paralympic* athletes in their rigorous training regimens.

These tours provide an intimate look at the facilities that help shape champions. The proud legacy of *Colorado's Olympic and Paralympic* training is evident here, where hopefuls are nurtured every day.

The **Garden of the Gods** was a gift from the Charles Perkins Family to the city of Colorado Springs back in 1909, under the conditions that the park *"should be maintained as a free and public park forever."*[8,9] If you're looking to be awed by some incredible rock formations, make your way to the *Garden of the Gods*.

Located roughly an hour and a half from DIA, if you manage to avoid the rush hour traffic, this natural wonder is easily accessible, and a short scenic drive from the *U.S. Air Force Academy*.

My favorite formation within this stunning park is the *Kissing Camels*. True to its name, this beautiful sandstone red rock formation resembles two camels locked in a tender kiss.

The *Garden of the Gods* is not only a geological marvel but also a testament to the beauty that nature can sculpt over time. Whether you're an avid photographer, a nature enthusiast, or simply looking for a peaceful escape, this park is a must-visit destination that offers breathtaking views and a serene atmosphere.

Have I mentioned that the wildlife in Colorado is unbelievable? You never know what you're going to encounter on a trail. Today, we spotted a herd of bighorn sheep in the brush just off the trail.

These magnificent creatures are the largest wild sheep in North America. Muscular males can weigh over 300 pounds and stand over three feet tall at the shoulder. It's important to remember that these are wild animals, and we are visitors in their territory. We must respect their space and observe them from a safe distance to ensure their habitat remains undisturbed and we remain unharmed.

At the base of Pikes Peak in El Paso County lies the charming town of **Manitou Springs,** a perfect blend of natural beauty and quaint charm. Manitou Springs is a picturesque town that offers more than just its proximity to the awe-inspiring *Garden of the Gods*. After marveling at the majestic rock formations, visitors can stroll through the enchanting streets to discover a variety of delightful dining options. For those with a sweet tooth, visiting the local candy shops is a must, providing the perfect sugary indulgence to cap off a day of adventure.

The town itself exudes a quaint, mountain-town atmosphere that complements the natural wonders surrounding it. Whether you're drawn to the area for its breathtaking landscapes or the cozy, small-town feel, Manitou Springs promises an experience that will capture your heart and create memories to cherish. I reflect on childhood memories of visiting **Patsy's Candies** and picking out my favorite taffy. The sweet shop first opened in 1903 and is still handcrafting candies.[10]

Another one of Colorado's 14'ers, **Pikes Peak Mountain** is a true marvel and a landmark that has historically guided settlers with their wooden wagons westward. It's a mountain steeped in stories, including the one my mom often recounts about the time she hiked it. They set out for a nice afternoon to enjoy the weather, but what they found instead was that they were lost. Without water and proper hiking shoes, they faced the dangers that Colorado's summits are known for cold, darkness, and an extreme sense of vulnerability when unprepared.

They reached the summit only to find the gift shop closed, leaving them without the means to call for help or a way down from the chilly mountaintop. Fortuitously, a kind ranger found them and brought them back to safety. Cell phone service is spotty and may be nonexistent in the higher mountains.

There are a few ways to reach the top of Pikes Peak, which looms at 14,115 feet, about 8,000 feet above Colorado Springs. For avid hikers, there's a trail to the top. But you don't have to be a hiker to experience the summit—you can also drive.

In my opinion, the best way to savor the summit's breathtaking views is by taking the **Cog Railway**. Opening in 1891, it's known for being the world's **highest-cog**, railroad, reaching the sky at a whopping 8.9 miles long.[11] Relax and take in the sights of wildlife, pine, and aspen trees as the train climbs to the summit.

. . .

*Tip:*

*Remember to bring your jacket; it's chilly, and the air is thin at the top. On my last visit, it was in the high 90s when we set out. I didn't give the temperature much thought until we started the ascent and encountered the cold at the summit. The expensive souvenir blanket we purchased wasn't just for the memories—it was a necessity. To this day, it reminds us of the brisk temperature, even during the brief 10-minute stop at the top, and that we still had an hour and ten minutes left on the ride down. You can also spend more time hiking and take a later train down.*

Located in the same parking area as the Cog, the ***Manitou Springs Incline*** is a hike I've yet to tackle, but it has inspired me through a high school friend. She and her daughter run up this staircase, which ascends an additional 2,000 feet in elevation. If you stand on the top you will be at an elevation of 8,500.

I have no intention of ever running it, and I'm not even sure if I'll make it to the top of the more than 2,744 uneven steps. If you're considering

this challenge, plan ahead; reservations are required, and they fill up quickly.[12] A quick look at the website today shows that reservations are booked for the next 28 days. When it reopens on the first of next month it will be on a first-come, first-served basis.

You can book for free, but parking costs around $14 for four hours. Keep in mind this is the off-season; I'm not sure if summer fees are higher. Once again, pack lots of water. Some hikers can complete this in 30 minutes, but for me, I'm sure it's going to take closer to three maybe four hours.

Don't forget to stop in at ***The North Pole*** to see ***Santa's Workshop***. This park brings back so many memories. Our children, especially our oldest, loved this park growing up. She had wide eyes as she watched the elves make toys. Glassblowing was one of my favorites. Enjoy the food, amusement park rides, and even a visit with Santa. Keep in mind that Santa is tired after delivering packages around the world on Christmas Eve and closes the shop for his holiday break from Christmas Day to mid-May.[13]

Fast cars, heart-pounding speeds, over 156 turns, and the rush of adrenaline as they race to the summit—it's all part of the thrill you can witness in Colorado at ***The Race to the Clouds***.[14] Drivers race to the sky as they conquer Colorado's summit heights in a race car. Just thinking about the race cars zooming up the winding roads of Pikes Peak with tires inches from the cliffs gets my heart racing. Also known as *"Broadmoor Pikes Peak International Hill Climb"*, *The Race to the Clouds* is an event that combines the beauty of the mountains with the excitement of motorsport, and it's definitely one of the items on Steve's and my bucket lists.

Do you like exploring the enigmatic depths of dark caves? If the answer is yes, then Colorado is a destination you can't miss. The state boasts an array of caves nestled throughout the Rocky Mountains, each with their unique features and history. One cave that has left a lasting impression on me is the ***Cave of the Winds*** in Manitou Springs.

I've taken the tour several times over the years, and it was there, as a child, that I first encountered absolute darkness. I thought I knew what darkness was, but when the tour guide switched off all the lights in the chilly, damp cavern, I quickly realized I had never experienced true blackness before. It's hard to imagine how the boys credited with discovering the cave back in 1881 managed to navigate such an environment.[15] The cave is adorned with incredible stalactites and stalagmites, adding to its otherworldly ambiance.

Beyond the Cave of the Winds, there are also numerous cave and gold mining tours available across the state, offering a deeper insight into the history of gold panning and mining. These tours provide a unique perspective on Colorado's rich mining heritage and are a testament to the adventurous spirit of those who sought fortune in the heart of the mountains.

While I have not personally embarked on the hike up to the **Broadmoor Seven Falls**, the prospect remains tempting. The climb, often compared to ascending a 17-story building via *224 steps*, is a challenge that our group did not take on—our collective energy reserves were not primed for such an endeavor.[16] Nonetheless, we embraced an alternative experience by visiting the falls at night, where we were greeted by the stunning sight of cascading waters illuminated against the dark sky. This was an adventure that was equally breathtaking in its own right.

I've heard from others that at the summit, there are tranquil pools where you can swim and bask on the sun-warmed rocks—a perfect reward for those who conquer the climb. Contrary to some expectations, these are not hot springs; the waters are refreshingly cool/cold, fed by the runoff from melting snow. For many, this natural chill is a welcome respite after the exertion of the hike, offering a rejuvenating finale to the journey.

**The Broadmoor Resort** is a symphony of splendor, elegance, and historical charm nestled in Colorado Springs. This legendary *Diamond resort* boasts the longest-running Forbes 5-star status globally, and its reputation speaks for itself.[17] The East Course, renowned for its golfing excellence, is frequently ranked among the best in the nation. Guests can also stroll the immaculate grounds, taking in the awe-inspiring views of Pikes Peak and Cheyenne Mountain.

**The Broadmoor Golf Club** is a prestigious course that provides lush greens and *luxurious amenities*. The world-class course has hosted several USGA championships since 1959. Because the resort is a private club, you must either be a guest or be invited by a member to play.

What truly sets *The Broadmoor* apart is its rich tapestry of history. It has served as a backdrop for a couple of films, including the classic *Perry Mason* and *Ice Castles*. An interesting anecdote I discovered while researching for this chapter, involves *George W. Bush*, who experienced a pivotal moment at this historic resort. In 1986, after waking up with a hangover amidst the majestic Colorado landscape, he made the life-altering decision to quit drinking. Roughly 15 years later, he would become the 43rd President of the United States.[18]

The dining experience at the resort is nothing short of extraordinary, with a plethora of restaurants to choose from. I've had the privilege of touring the bustling kitchen and savoring a meal prepared by the talented chef—a testament to the culinary delights that await every guest. It's hard to imagine anything on the menu that wouldn't be delectable.

Offering a wide range of reasonable pricing depending on the season, today you might find accommodations on the property for under $400 a night. I even found a couple of specials for under $350. Of course, suites and rooms with more superior views command a premium, with prices reaching around $900 and higher. For comparison, a stay at a Holiday Inn could range from $100 to $225 per night, varying by room choice and location.

A Zoological treasure on the mountainside, discover the wonders of the animal kingdom at **Cheyenne Mountain Zoo**, where learning and adventure go hand in hand. As a zoologist's park, it's no surprise that it's been ranked as one of the top zoos in the country by *USA Today 10Best* and *TripAdvisor*. [19,20] I can attest it's one of the finest zoos I've ever visited.

Prepare for an invigorating hike, as this unique zoo is nestled on the side of a mountain. Home to exotic animals and hands-on exhibits, the zoo offers an educational journey like no other. Spend a full day exploring and learning as you trek from exhibit to exhibit, each encounter promising new insights and unforgettable experiences.

When the holiday season arrives, the zoo sparkles with an extra layer of magic. The annual tradition of holiday lights transforms the grounds into an illuminated wonderland, adding a festive flair to the already captivating experience. This special time of year is a highlight for visitors, combining the joy of wildlife with the enchanting atmosphere of the season's festivities. Cheyenne Mountain Zoo is not just a place to see animals; it's a destination that combines the thrill of nature with the joy of discovery.

Walk among the clouds at *the **Royal Gorge Bridge***. Located in Fremont County near Cañon City, the bridge is suspended 1,000 feet high above the Arkansas River. The *Royal Gorge Bridge* was a marvel that captured my imagination at the tender age of 11 when I rode across it in our family minivan. Back then, it reigned as the highest bridge in the world, and although it lost that title in 2001, it retains the distinction of being the world's highest suspension bridge. The memory of a girls' outing with our mom is etched in my mind—crossing those 1,257 wooden planks, I was gripped by a thrilling fear of the vast expanse below.[21]

From the bridge, the ***Arkansas River*** seems a world away, with whitewater rafters reduced to the size of tiny ants by the dizzying height. For those who wish to explore the depths of the canyon, the journey is well worth it. There's a charming gift shop at the end of the walk, offering souvenirs. For the more adventurous souls, the bridge offers the chance to zip line across the canyon, providing an adrenaline rush like no other. The red cable cars offer a more tranquil passage, gliding smoothly across the gorge or descending the mountain, allowing visitors to take in the breathtaking views at a leisurely pace.

Whether you're drawn to the area for its breathtaking landscapes, or the cozy small-town feel, Colorado Springs and Manitou Springs promise an experience that will capture your heart and create memories to cherish.

*Tip:*
*The river is cold. If you're planning on a rafting trip, expect to get wet. I was glad I bought women's swim trunks; they dried quickly. My girlfriend, on the other hand, wore jean shorts and was freezing all day.*

# CHAPTER 6

# THE AMERICAN SPIRIT BISHOP CASTLE

## A TESTAMENT TO DEDICATION AND CREATIVITY

If you wander off-the-beaten-path, somewhere 9,000 feet above sea level, is a little plot of land that has left its mark on Colorado's history. At just 15 years old, Jim Bishop had already saved enough money from various odd jobs to purchase 2.5 of acres of land for $450 in the late 1960s. This hidden gem, now known as *Bishop Castle*, is nestled in the south-central part of Colorado, just off State Highway 165.[1]

The castle stands as a testament to Jim Bishop's unwavering dedication and perseverance, as he spent an astonishing forty-four years constructing this magnificent structure, handling each piece of stone numerous times.[2]

The awe-inspiring Bishop Castle, standing tall at around 16 stories, is not only a marvel of stone but also features intricate ironwork throughout. Visitors can explore the castle's many lookout points, which offer breathtaking views of the surrounding landscape.

You can find striking and unique elements at every corner, even a fire-breathing dragon that watches over the castle – a testament to Jim Bishop's creativity and craftsmanship. This remarkable creature adds an element of fantasy to the already enchanting atmosphere of the castle, captivating the imagination of all who witness its fiery display.

Jim Bishop's unwavering commitment to sharing his dream with others was evident in his decision to open the castle doors to the public without charging an admission fee. With a firm belief in the goodwill of his visitors, he opted for a donation-based system, placing a box on the grounds for those who wished to contribute to the ongoing construction. This honor system quickly became the lifeblood of the castle's continuous growth, as the generosity of those who appreciated Jim's incredible work funded the project.

This year, at the age of 79, Jim Bishop has retired. It seems that his new dream is to travel to all the places he hasn't seen around Colorado. I'm a little disappointed that I never made it to the castle to witness him working on his dream with his own two hands. Visiting *Bishop Castle* is still on my bucket list. The allure of the castle has always fascinated me, and I've been told that it's one of Colorado's overlooked masterpieces.

# CHAPTER 7

# DUNES OF WONDER

## DISCOVERING THE MAGIC OF COLORADO'S ENCHANTING DESERT OASIS

Colorado is landlocked with no beaches, but we have picturesque sand. The ***Great Sand Dunes*** is one of Colorado's gems, famous for its expansive dunes. Ready for some adventure? Let's go sandboarding, sand sledding, and you can even ski! It may sound wild, but you can do it right on the dune field away from vegetated areas at The ***Great Sand Dunes National Park***, home to the tallest dunes in North America and one of the most intricate dune systems in the world. The park offers endless fun and is a marvel of Colorado's natural beauty.[1]

The park is open year-round 365 days. You can camp under the stars in the national park from April to October, remember to book your spot up to six months in advance as they tend to fill up quickly!

There's no lodging inside the park other than campsites. But don't worry—a short 35-minute drive to the small town of **Mosca** or the larger city of **Alamosa** has you covered.

You can capture the beautiful moments best at sunrise and sunset. Arrive early enough, and you might even dodge the entrance fee. Though smaller than other parks, a couple of hours here lets you see it all or take longer to enjoy a leisurely lunch or marvel at the peaks of these sandy mountains.

A sand dunes oasis is worth exploring. After a day of adventure, unwind with a soothing dip in the geothermal waters. ***The Sand Dunes Recreation*** hot spring maintains a cozy temperature between 98 and 101 degrees. There is also a separate pool for adults aged 25 and older, where you can enjoy temperatures of 105 to 107 degrees.[2] Additionally, like in many mountain communities, you'll find an array of hot springs to choose from, ensuring a perfectly tranquil soak.

ATVs and 4-wheeling are off-limits in the national park, but plenty of places nearby offer tours and rentals for ATVs, UTVs, Razors, and even Jeeps. I've heard incredible things about Razor Adventures, it's definitely on my bucket list.

Make sure to stay safe. Remember, at 8,200 feet, the dunes can be deceiving. Summer temps average 75-85 degrees, but the sand can reach

150 degrees. Sunscreen is a must, even when it's not hot, due to the high altitude.

Hike in the early morning or late afternoon, wear closed-toed shoes or boots, and protect your dog's paws from the heat. Like always, staying hydrated will help with altitude sickness.

This one has been on my bucket list for over a decade; it's time to get it checked off.

# CHAPTER 8

# MESA VERDE

## AN UNFORGETTABLE JOURNEY
## KINDLING THE FLAMES OF CURIOSITY

Our family's excursion to **Mesa Verde National Park** remains one of the most incredible trips we've ever taken. [1] Picture this, a family camping adventure with our new pop-up camper, a toddler, her four-year-old brother, and girls aged around 9 and 10.

Our original destination was the Grand Canyon, but a last-minute decision at the exit rerouted us to a campground in Southern Colorado. The drive proved unexpectedly challenging due to road construction delays and a rockslide that resulted in a lengthy wait for a detour, ultimately leading us on a nerve-wracking journey over mountainous terrain. Although my husband's experience in towing aircraft meant we weren't initially concerned, the steep cliffs and loose rocks tested our nerves, especially with our precious cargo on board.

Despite the previous day's tension, our children awoke early, their singing voices echoing through the campsite as I fetched water. They were oblivious to the fact that the real adventure was yet to begin.

### Ancestral Pueblo People & Cliff Palace

Visiting the **_Cliff Palace_**, where the Ancestral Pueblo People once lived, had been a dream of mine since childhood. Now, I was thrilled to share this experience with my children. For those with a fear of heights, even viewing the palace from a distance is awe-inspiring. The tour began easily enough, with all the kids handling the walk well and our toddler comfortably nestled in the backpack.

Seeing the world through their eyes was extraordinary. Our oldest was lost in wonder, pondering the lives of those who once inhabited these cliffside dwellings, while her sister tested limits, drawn to the edges, much to my anxiety. Our four-year-old, curious, and eager, questioned why he couldn't light a fire in the pit. These were some of the most incredible views I have ever seen.

The tour's *132 steps* and *32-foot ladder* were a breeze for the family. However, the *60-foot ascent* on the cliffside, the 3rd ladder, and the final 17-foot ladder climb were a little terrifying. Reflecting on the experience, I'm astonished by the Ancestral Pueblo people's daily lives. This journey through Mesa Verde was more than just a trip—it was a testament to the resilience of families, both ancient and modern, and a profound connection to history that we will never forget. And don't worry, our little fire-maker, after collecting timber, was able to start our campfire at camp with some help from his dad.

Upon arrival, I was somewhat let down to see just a large concrete slab marking the intersection of the four states, complete with benches around its perimeter to sit. There were a couple of modest wooden booths serving as gift shops with Native American crafts.

However, any initial disappointment quickly gave way to amusement. It was entertaining to have our kids stand in each of the states—

Colorado, Arizona, Utah, and New Mexico—all at once while enjoying snow cones.

This simple yet unique experience allowed us to savor a moment of lighthearted fun, as we each claimed a corner in a different state, creating a fond memory at the only *quadripoin*t in the United States.

CHAPTER 9

# RED ROCKS AMPHITHEATER

## POWER OF MOTHER NATURE
## HARMONIZING WITH ICONIC
## PERFORMANCES

**Red Rocks Amphitheater** stands as an awe-inspiring music venue, its grandeur unparalleled. Carved by the hands of time over 300 million years, this majestic rock formation is a sight to behold.[1]

I vividly recall my first concert there in 1993, with the legendary *Bon Jovi* taking the stage—an experience forever ingrained in my memory. Situated about 10 miles from Denver in Morrison, *Colorado, Red Rocks* is more than a mere concert location; it's a natural marvel offering breathtaking views that sweep across the landscape, captivating visitors with its beauty and acoustic excellence.

The amphitheater is nestled within a unique geological formation of towering red sandstone rocks, which not only create an unforgettable visual spectacle but also contribute to the venues renowned acoustics. The setting is so picturesque that it becomes a destination in itself, attracting visitors even when there isn't a concert scheduled.

For those looking to stay active, *Red Rocks* doubles as an open-air gym. The amphitheater's seating area, with its vast array of bleachers, becomes a popular workout spot where fitness enthusiasts can be found running the steps, an exercise that's as challenging as it is rewarding given the altitude and the natural beauty of the area.

I wish I could have captured the amazing stage that so many performers have left their mark on. However, it was all blocked off due to construction. We talked to some construction workers who asked us to remind our readers to stay on the marked trails. It seems many people do not follow the signs and cross into taped-off areas. The signs are there for your safety.

There was also a museum that showcased the history of the park and all the famous artists who have played there. Both parking and entry to the museum and the venue were free that day, as there were no concerts scheduled. It's wonderful that people can enjoy the museum and outdoor space without incurring a charge.

During our photoshoot at *Red Rocks,* it was inspiring to see so many people utilizing this magnificent space for their workouts—a shoutout to all those dedicated runners who added such vibrant energy to the backdrop of our shoot. Red Rocks truly is a multipurpose venue that epitomizes Colorado's spirit of outdoor living and cultural richness.

# CHAPTER 10

# TEATIME & BOULDER ADVENTURES

## SIPPING TEA TO SCALING PEAKS

Nestled up against the Rocky Mountains, **Boulder**, Colorado is brimming with activities for every kind of visitor. The distinctive Flatirons give this picturesque city an unmistakable skyline. In the heart of the city, you'll find an array of delectable dining options on almost every corner. For those who enjoy open-air shopping, the **Pearl Street Mall** offers a unique experience with its shopping microbreweries and food.

Boulder is also renowned for its outdoor activities. With just a short drive, you can witness people scaling the mountain cliffs, a testament to the city's vibrant rock-climbing culture. **Boulder Canyon** distinguishes itself from other climbing spots in the region due to its predominantly granite composition.[1] While much of Boulder and the Front Range are characterized by sandstone or gneiss formations, the granite found in Boulder Canyon offers climbers a more robust and reliable surface.

This solid rock type is known for its strength and resistance to breakage, providing climbers with peace of mind as they tackle the various ascents the canyon has to offer. The durability of granite not only makes for safer climbs but also contributes to the area's wide range of climbing routes, appealing to climbers who appreciate both the challenge and security of this hardy stone.

Another nearby park is **Eldorado Canyon State Park**, where you'll find stunning backdrops sure to take your breath away. Make sure to check their site, as some of the climbing spots are closed during the year due to the nesting of our state raptors, the **American bald eagles**.[2]

**Boulder Reservoir** is a popular spot for boating enthusiasts in the Boulder area, offering a spacious and scenic setting for a variety of water activities.[3] With its expansive surface area, the reservoir accommodates sailboats, motorboats, kayaks, and paddle-boards, making it a versatile destination for those looking to spend a day on the water. The reservoir's calm waters are ideal for both leisurely boating and more exhilarating water sports. Park permits are required and can be purchased at the gate. In addition to boating, Boulder Reservoir is a haven for other recreational activities. Its sandy beaches and picnic areas provide the perfect backdrop for a family outing or a relaxing day in the sun. Cyclists and runners can take advantage of the trails that surround the reservoir, enjoying the stunning views as they get their workout in.

For anglers, **South Boulder Creek**, which feeds into the reservoir, is considered one of the most consistent fly-fishing spots in the area. Its clear waters and abundant fish populations offer a rewarding experience for both novice and experienced fly fishers.[4] If you are new to the area, several fishing guides are in the area who will take you to their honey holes.

Fun Fact: Boulder is home to the popular tea company **Celestial Seasonings**, where you can embark on a tour for around $5.[5] Not only is the tour affordable, but it also includes a complimentary sampling of their diverse teas at the Tea Bar. Whether you're a tea aficionado or simply looking for a relaxing experience, this is a delightful way to spend an afternoon. This one has been on my bucket list for over a decade; it's time to get it checked off.

A Hub of rivalry and culture can be felt in the Mile High. Boulder is not just a haven for outdoor enthusiasts and foodies; it's also the home of the **University of Colorado Boulder (CU)**, the rival of **Colorado State University (CSU)**.[6,7] The *CU* campus is a thriving hub of arts, music, and culture, deeply intertwined with the scientific community. The vibrant atmosphere on campus is palpable, with a rich blend of academic pursuits and creative expression.

Another amazing activity for cyclists, BMX enthusiasts and moun-tain bikers is ***Valmont Bike Park***.[8] Spanning 42 acres, the park offers trails for all skill levels, complete with shelters, picnic areas, and a dog park. You can spend the day watching riders jump their bikes and whisk through the trails. I had a great time on the beginner trails and enjoyed watching Steve and my kids tackle the more expert jumping paths.

Visitors and locals alike can feel the dynamic energy that emanates from the university, contributing to Boulder's unique and eclectic charm. Overall, the Boulder area is a paradise for those who appreciate breathtaking views and a multitude of outdoor activities. Whether you're casting a line in South Boulder Creek, scaling the heights of Boulder Canyon, or enjoying a day in one of Boulder's amazing parks, the natural beauty, and adventures of Colorado are at your fingertips.

# CHAPTER 11

# OFF-ROAD ADVENTURES

## A FOUR-WHEELER'S HEAVEN ON THE BACK ROADS

Growing up in Colorado, I had never been 4-wheeling in the mountains. My friends think it's crazy and can't believe I missed out on the experience growing up. But now, I'm crossing off items from my Colorado bucket list and hoping to return next summer. The state's abundant off-roading trails offer a one-of-a-kind thrill.

You can rent Jeeps and four-wheelers at many tourist towns in Colorado like Estes Park, Winter Park, and more. My buddy and best friend took Steve and me up on the trails this year. Over the summer, we tackled many of them.

Starting near **Arapaho National Forest**, we picked a trail from an app called *AllTrails*. **Dakota Hill SE OHV Trail** was our first choice, and our journey quickly led us into dense forests and up steep inclines. The interconnected trails provided endless entertainment, and as we climbed, the trails opened to amazing views of the mountain valleys.

The panoramic mountain views captivated us. This area offers trails for all skill levels and vehicle types. There are online Jeep groups that discuss trail conditions and what to expect. We took the moderate trail and had a special experience with the doors off. Steep rocks made us feel like we were sideways at times.

It was so much fun and we took a break for a picnic at the top. We hiked around a little at a couple of the wide spots of the trail. We were not in a rush and took our time. It took us a little over two hours to finish the 10-mile trail. Here are some tips for those planning an off-roading adventure in the Colorado Mountains.

### Packing list

- **Lip Balm**: It might not be part of your daily routine, but the dry Colorado air can lead to chapped lips, especially at higher altitudes. If you are in a Jeep with the doors off, or a topless vehicle, lip balm is a must. It's a small item, but you'll be grateful to have it in your daypack.

- **Skin Hydration**: Colorado is dry and we all needed to apply something later that night. While our friends used the usual lotion, we opted for coconut oil which we feel hydrates us better at altitude. Not to mention, the nutty smell reminds us of our time in the tropics.

- **Pack a Lunch and Snacks**: There's no need to rush through the beautiful landscapes. Nuts and sunflower seeds are a high-protein option that travels well. Prepare a lunch, you can always find a scenic pull-off to enjoy your meal while soaking in the breathtaking views.

- **Use an Off-Road App**: Technology can be a great aid. Off-road apps often contain valuable information from other travelers about the trails. Read reviews and trail conditions before you set out, as some paths can be steep with large ruts, requiring you to navigate almost sideways on rocks.

- **Offline Maps/Paper Map**: Cell service can be spotty in the mountains, so it's important to download maps ahead of time or carry a paper map. Having access to offline maps can be crucial for navigation when you're out of service range. If your vehicle should fail, it is important to know which direction is shortest to get help. Additionally, cell phones can run out of charge or break, so knowing your way out is critical.

- **Emergency Kit**: Always carry an emergency kit equipped with water, a snakebite kit, and some non-perishable food. It's better to be over-prepared than under-prepared in case of an unexpected situation.

- **Dress in Layers**: Mountain weather can be unpredictable. You might start in shorts and a shirt, but it's wise to pack sweaters, stocking caps/beanies, and heavy jackets. Temperatures can drop quickly, especially as you gain altitude, so having layers will keep you comfortable throughout the trip.

- **Shovel:** A sturdy shovel is a must-have; it's essential for digging out tires if you find yourself stuck in a tricky spot. We have found a shovel to be useful on many occasions.
- **Tell someone where you are going:** Stuff happens and should your vehicle break down, severe weather conditions, or injuries occur, it is important that you can be found should you be stuck in the mountains unexpectedly.
- **Sunscreen:** Even on cloudy days sunscreen is a must. At 5200+ feet above sea level, Colorado is close to the sun and the air is thin, burning happens quickly.

With the proper preparations, a day four-wheeling through the Rocky Mountains can be an exhilarating and breathtaking experience. If it's not there already, this is a must-have for your bucket list.

# CHAPTER 12

# FROM GOLD RUSH TO BLACKJACK RUSH

## EXPLORING COLORADO'S HISTORIC TOWNS & CASINOS

L ocated in the mountains of Colorado, are two historic towns that offer a variety of activities for visitors. These towns are known for their casinos, but there are also plenty of free and cheap things to do for those on a budget.

Visitors can explore the museums, galleries, and landmarks that these towns have to offer. If you're planning a trip to **Black Hawk** or **Central City**, you're in for a treat. It's about a 4-minute drive between the two mountain towns. In this chapter, we'll focus on the top things to do, including a couple of my favorite casinos, as well as my top three places to stay and the reasons they stand out. Additionally, for the foodies, I'll share some culinary highlights that promise to make your visit even more delightful.

For those interested in history, the two towns have many original buildings. Visitors can also take advantage of the free shuttle bus between the two towns, which provides easy access to all the attractions.

On the way to these towns, we usually make a stop in the quaint mountain town of **Lyons**. Lyons boasts a few small shops and even a charming ice cream parlor. It's also an ideal spot for a bathroom break, as it's a bit of a drive before you encounter another stop.

One of our favorite pitstops is **Spirit Hound Distillers** in Lyons. When we last stopped by, the new addition had just been finished.[1] They let us check it out, but they were not yet serving from the new addition. I'm sure it's open by now and let me tell you, it's as cool as the designs that have been on display over the years. Although it is a distillery that my husband claims makes very tasty Colorado whiskey, I can't wait to stop back in and have another Bloody Mary.

We usually stop on the way up the mountains, so to me, a Bloody Mary seems more appropriate than whiskey. You can also see the distillery's iconic all-copper pot still, from the bar.

When exploring Colorado, it's interesting to note that bartenders often rinse the beer glass with water to make it more slippery, minimizing the friction when the beer fills it; this minimizes the foamy head. Additionally, many places will let you try a sample before you order, allowing you to test the flavors and avoid ending up with a drink that is not to your liking.

Another one of our favorite stops as we head up the hill is **Knotted Root Brewing Company** in Nederland.[2] They have a patio and there's always something new on tap.

Once you arrive in Black Hawk, it's time to get the good times rolling. First up is **Horseshoe Casino** formally known as the *Isle Casino* and Hotel, this is a Caesars Entertainment property. Don't forget to get your player's card because points here count toward the Las Vegas casino, and vice versa. The gaming complex is one of Colorado's top gaming destinations. With slot machines that are constantly changing and dozens of table games, plus a high-spin slot area, there's something for every adult.

Gambling isn't the only thing to do at Horseshoe. The casino also offers a variety of dining options. I usually enjoy the breakfast burrito in the new **Brew Brothers** sports bar at the top of the escalators. Just like the machines and hotel names, the restaurant names are constantly changing, but the burrito has remained the same.

Right next to *Brew Brothers* is a little cafe and grab-and-go food mart that's open twenty-four hours a day called **Dash Cafe**. In addition to being able to grab a bag of chips or some candy, they serve a variety of takeout foods such as sandwiches, hamburgers, and salads. My first time having *Pho* was there, and I loved it. There are also a couple of cool food vending machines in the back part of the casino. I haven't had the opportunity to eat from any of them yet, but it's on my bucket list just to see how the food tastes.

On our last few trips, due to late notice, the *Horseshoe Casino* was fully booked, so we made reservations at their sister hotel **Lady Luck Casino** located next door. I liked the rooms at both casinos; however, I feel the *Horseshoe casino* was a bit more upscale. It's worth mentioning that neither of them has a pool.

Located across the street is the **Monarch Casino Resort & Spa**. This independent resort is a premier destination for gaming, entertainment, and dining. The casino floor is bustling with a diverse selection of slot machines and table games, providing ample opportunity to test your luck and enjoy the thrill of the game. Beyond gaming, Monarch boasts a range of dining experiences, with a buffet standing out as an award-winning option where you can indulge in unlimited prime rib, Italian and Mexican bars, as well as, seafood like sushi. Note: The crab legs and lobster tail are not all you can eat; instead, you get tickets to hand to the server. There is so much food that we have never used all of our tickets during the many feasts.

The dessert section at *Monarch Casino* is a paradise for those with a sweet tooth. During our last visit, it was the crowning jewel of our party. Imagine a spread where delicate cupcakes beckon with their swirls of frosting, each bite a burst of flavor. The gelato, smooth and rich, offers a cool respite, with an array of flavors to suit every palate. For a touch of whimsy, there's cotton candy—fluffy, sweet clouds that dissolve delightfully on the tongue.

The pièce de resistance strawberries were freshly dipped in chocolate, prepared by their skilled chef. Each strawberry is a perfect balance of fruit and decadence, the chocolate shell giving way to the juicy berry within. It's clear that the dessert offerings are not just an afterthought; they're a key part of the experience, crafted with care to ensure every guest leaves with a sweet memory of their celebration.

We took a free tour of the **Monarch Casino Resort & Spa**, which was voted one of the **top hotel spas in the nation** by *USA Today readers*.[3] Touring the world-class spa was as easy as just stopping in to ask. The place is amazing, featuring everything from ice rooms and a snow shower to hot saunas and mineral rock rooms for meditation. They also offer private and couples massages.

   A Toast to Love and Bison Ribeye.

It was an exhilarating evening celebrating the marriage engagement of our friends, who had been raving about the **Monarch Chophouse.** The Chophouse has a reputation for having the best steaks in Black Hawk and some would say, Colorado. I was eager to put that claim to the test. I had never tried a Bison bone-in ribeye before, but I must say, they knocked it out of the park. The service was impeccable, and the staff even brought out tasters of top-shelf whiskey for the boys.

For us ladies, the waiter helped us choose a wine out of *Napa Valley* called *Roots Run Deep - Educated Guess Reserve Red Blend 2019* to compliment our steaks. Incredible wine, plus the best piece of meat I have ever tasted in Colorado made this a meal to remember. Our desserts were prepared table side, adding an extra touch of magic to an already special night. To my friends who have since tied the knot, congratulations and thank you for letting us be a part of your memorable celebration.

Next up is rooftop relaxing. Monarch Resort is a haven of comfort and luxury. I particularly love staying here for the rooftop pool and hot tub, which offer a peaceful escape with stunning views—a perfect way to unwind after a day of excitement. Whether you're there to gamble, dine, or simply relax, Monarch Casino Resort & Spa is a destination that promises a memorable experience. Note, if you are traveling with any children or people under 21, the pool opens and closes early for adult-only swimming.

The diner at **Bally's** is where greasy goodness reigns supreme. Tucked away behind the poker tables at Bally's there's a little-known kitchen that serves up the best diner delights in Black Hawk. This modest hole-in-the-wall eatery is a secret among taste enthusiasts, offering a front-row seat to poker tournament action if you time your visit right. During our twenty-plus ascents up the hill, our group has sampled nearly every item on the menu, and each dish has proven to be praise-worthy. Our favorites, the ones we keep coming back for, include the hearty breakfast sandwich, the cheesy chicken quesadilla, and the crispy tater tots, perfectly paired with a side of green chili for dipping.

Bally's is also home to my husband's favorite table game, Super Six.

I must admit it is the only table game I have won. I was able to walk away up a couple hundred dollars. It is easy to learn and the dealers and other players are usually open to give advice. You are playing against the house and not other players. Some dealers prefer their tips in the form of a bet on their behalf to potentially multiply their tip.

***Ameristar Casino Resort Spa Black Hawk*** *i*s where one of my most memorable nights was spent. We indulged in their *Spa King Suite*, which exceeded our expectations. The suite was luxurious, providing the ideal setting for an evening of entertainment with friends. The next morning, I found pure relaxation as I soaked in the in-room jetted tub, the gentle massage of the water jets complementing the warmth from the flickering fireplace. As I reclined in the bath, the view of the majestic mountainside outside my window was a peaceful backdrop, creating a moment of tranquility that I still cherish to this day. You can also take a dip in the Olympic-sized pool and indoor hot tub. Outside, there are fire pits and an additional hot tub.

If you're interested in learning more about the history of Black Hawk and the surrounding area, the ***Gilpin History Museum*** is a great place to start. The museum features exhibits on the history of mining, transportation, and daily life in the area. You can also learn about the *Native American tribes* who lived in the region and see artifacts from their cultures. The museum is housed in a historic building and offers guided tours for visitors.

Are you looking for cheap things to do in Black Hawk & Central City? Visiting Black Hawk and Central City doesn't have to break the bank. And if you have already deposited most of your money in the casinos, there is still fun to be had. There are plenty of activities that won't cost you an arm and a leg.

### Affordable and Free Things to Do

**1. Take a scenic driv**e - The drive to Black Hawk and Central City is beautiful, especially during the fall when the leaves are changing colors. Choose a direction and take a leisurely drive to enjoy the scenery. Don't forget to turn on your GPS so you can find your way back.

**2. Visit the *Teller House*** – Over 150 years old, the ***Teller House*** in Central City is a historic hotel that was once a popular spot for miners and prospectors. You can take a tour of the hotel for a small fee.

**3. Go hiking** - The scenic mountains offer a variety of hiking trails for all skill levels, ranging from easy walks to challenging hikes. The trails offer stunning views of the surrounding area, including the city of Black Hawk and the ***Rocky Mountains*** of ***San Juan National Forest***. Make sure to bring your camera to capture the breathtaking scenery! Pack a picnic and spend the day exploring the great outdoors.

**4. Visit the *Gilpin History Museum*** - The Gilpin History Museum in Central City is dedicated to preserving the history of the area. Admission is free, but donations are welcome.

**5. Take a brewery tour** - The small towns around these gambling towns have a few local breweries that offer tours and tastings.

**6. Historic sightseeing** - Take a stroll through the historic downtown area, which is home to many well-preserved Victorian buildings.

**7. Explore** - the ***Argo Gold Mine and Mill*** offers affordable tours descending into the depths of the historic mining site.

**8. Hike** - the trails in ***Golden Gate Canyon State Park***, which is located just a short 15-minute drive from Black Hawk, offers stunning views of the Rocky Mountains.

**9. *Central City Cemetery*** is about a 7-minute drive from the hotels in Black Hawk. We spent about an hour wandering through the cemetery. As a history buff, I found it incredibly fascinating. The graves date back to the pioneer days, and many of them are unmarked. The cemetery is huge, and we only explored the top part. From there we took in the breathtaking views.

These are just a few of the many affordable things to do in Black Hawk and Central City. With a little creativity, you can have a great time without spending a lot of money.

*Navigating Central City & Black Hawk*
*Driving Tip*

*If you're planning a visit to Central City and Black Hawk, it's worth noting that you don't necessarily need to drive there. Conveniently, there's a bus service from Denver that can take you directly to these historic towns. For those who prefer to drive, like we often do, ample parking is available in hotel garages. Once parked, you can easily get around by hopping on the complimentary red shuttle bus that services Black Hawk and Central City.*

# CHAPTER 13

# NOT GOLD IN THEM HILLS, IT'S GREEN

## CANNABIS CULTURE

On January 1, 2014, Colorado made history by becoming the first state in the U.S. to open its doors to the legal sale of recreational marijuana. The first retail cannabis shop to welcome customers was nestled in the historic mining town of Central City, situated in the scenic mountains west of Denver. As a Colorado resident, I'm quite familiar with dispensaries—they are a common sight, with one seemingly just down the street around the next corner. This particular shop held a unique allure, it was yet another destination to check off my travel bucket list.

During my visit, I had the opportunity to speak with one of the pioneering owners. She shared her personal story of operating the first recreational marijuana shop in the state, even showing us old photographs of the long lines that snaked around the building when they first opened.

Central City, along with the neighboring town of Black Hawk, forms Colorado's original gaming district. After the gold rush, the area experienced a downturn in fortunes, only to experience a resurgence in the 1990s with the introduction of casino gambling. The strategic decision to open the first recreational marijuana dispensary aimed to draw a new wave of tourists to the area.

*Annie's*, the trailblazing shop, secured its license on the last day of 2013 and kicked off sales bright and early at 8 a.m. on New Year's Day.[1] Eager cannabis enthusiasts queued in lengthy lines, eager to legally purchase everything from flower to edibles.

This grand opening catapulted Central City and Black Hawk into the spotlight as forerunners in the flourishing legal cannabis industry, garnering significant media attention and welcoming a host of new customers to the world of regulated marijuana sales. Since that day, Central City has fully embraced its role in cannabis tourism, with more dispensaries joining the historic downtown scene. Despite the growth, this original shop remains special—it's not just a dispensary but also a liquor and convenience store. The early foray of Central City into the recreational cannabis market has shown how the cannabis industry can breathe new life into former mining communities.

Did you know that many dispensaries offer free tours if you simply ask? They will guide you through the store, explaining the various strains and consumption methods, including edibles. With the right bud-tender, it can be a highly educational experience.

*Tip:*
*There is X-ray vision in DIA, and while Colorado is a state that celebrates cannabis, the Federal Aviation Administration (FAA) prohibits it, meaning you cannot legally carry cannabis products on a flight. Consume it or dispose of it before you arrive at the airport.*

# CHAPTER 14

# TAKE IT ALL OFF

## REVEALING THE HIDDEN HEALING POWERS MINERAL BATHS

We had an incredible time exploring **Idaho Springs** and the quaint mountain towns nearby. This charming town, established amid the gold rush of 1859, is a true gem nestled in the mountains. Its name, derived from the *Arapaho Indian* word *Edauhoe,* aptly translating to *Gem of the Mountains,* reflects the area's natural beauty and rich history.

Idaho Springs has many little gift shops that sell everything from soaps to Christmas tree decorations. You just have to walk the charming streets to find all your gifts and souvenirs. With all kinds of bar food choices, Idaho Springs offers a lot to foodies.

**Westbound & Down Brewing Company** is one of our favorites in Idaho Springs.[1] The waitress was so accommodating, she even opened the back patio for us to sit among the spas converted to look like whiskey barrels. They were heated, so the 15-degree weather outside was no problem for us. *Westbound & Down Brewing Company* had great food and drinks, plus the staff was amazing. On our next trip, we sat at the bar and learned they also honor our vets and first responders. I had the privilege of having a drink and conversing with two of them that day.

Another historical site we stopped at was **Indian Hot Springs**.[2] The main pool was under construction on one side, but we could still swim and play in it. In my opinion, it was warm, not hot, though we did find the hot water from the underground spring coming in on one side of the swimming pool.

The **GEO Thermal Caves** were an experience I was not expecting. When we decided to visit the caves, we were informed that we could not go with our male companions. Women and men were in two separate caves unless we booked a private room. Note the water temperature is a little cooler in the private rooms which are not as deep as the segregated caves. There was no question; I was eager to find out what was going on deep underground.

The thermal springs, accessed through passageways carved into the mountain in the early 1900s, emit waters with temperatures that consistently stay between 108 to 112 degrees Fahrenheit. These springs have been held in high regard as hallowed healing grounds by the *Ute* and *Arapaho* nations long before the passages were made, serving as a site for both spiritual practice and the mending of the sick and wounded.

Upon entering the first area, I encountered a locker room for changing. Right beside it was a peaceful room, and to my shock, it was filled with the sight of naked women deeply immersed in relaxation and meditation.

*Take It ALL OFF!* Standing there in my bikini, I felt unexpectedly over-dressed as I observed these figures spread out on the benches and chairs. The unexpected display of naked bodies was so startling that it caused my friend and me to completely miss the quiet sign. No one holds it against you if you keep it on, just keep in mind that the minerals are hard on the fabric of swimsuits, so don't wear your favorite one.

The dark cave carved out of the mountain and the hot pools made out of stone were just ahead. There were several baths, and as I stepped in, I reminded myself that our bodies should be cherished and there's nothing to be ashamed of—if you don't like it, don't look. The only way to experience travel in full force and be deeply touched by it is to be open to the opportunities placed in front of you.

I have taken in some of the most breathtaking hot springs in the world; one of the most glorious ones was in the jungles of Costa Rica, but at those locations, I was still in my bathing suit. This travel author was taking it all off. Another item checked off my bucket list. I thought I was going to do this in Japan; it never even crossed my mind that Colorado had a bathhouse.

It took me to a different world as the hot waters enveloped me, and my body absorbed the heat. My friend and I were lucky enough to have a tub to ourselves, but it wouldn't have bothered either of us if other women had joined in. After a long soak, we went back into the first room; it was cool with dim lighting. Laying back on a wooden rack, I joined the other ladies in what I would call a room full of meditation and relaxation. I have never been so in tune with my body, being open to the hot waters, and the healing minerals.

The separation of the caves and the nudity was a surprise, but it added a unique dimension to the experience—one that allowed for a kind of vulnerability among strangers that is rare and precious.

I can't wait to return. It may sound extraordinary, but I can personally testify to the medicinal qualities of these waters, which provided me with significant relief from pain and aided in my detoxification during this trip. As I emerged from the cave, feeling refreshed and more connected to myself, I couldn't help but reflect on the natural wonders that offer such healing experiences. The combination of the heat, the minerals, and the unique atmosphere had a profound effect on me, one that I'll carry with me long after the warmth of the waters has faded.

Another good hot spring that my aunt loves to visit is **Glenwood Springs**.[3] The water is so hot at a piping 122 degrees Fahrenheit that they cool it down before it enters the main pool to 104 degrees. You are sure to find a temperature you like in one of the 7 inviting pools.

There are so many healing hot mineral springs around this great state. As always, I recommend checking age limits, as many throughout the state have limited hours or do not allow kids at all. I love these hot springs and pools. They are always among my favorite activities!

# CHAPTER 15

# COLORADO'S YEAR-ROUND ALPINE PLAYGROUND

## BEYOND THE SKI SLOPES

T he ski scene in Colorado is a diverse mosaic, offering options for every preference and ensuring that the exhilarating rush of the descent is available to everyone who hears the mountains' wintry call.

Whether you're carving down a renowned run or savoring the charm of a local slope, Colorado's winter wonderland welcomes you with open arms. But skiing is not the only outdoor activity that these resorts offer.

These resorts offer year-round attractions in the majestic Rocky Mountains. Just west of our last location in Idaho Springs, you begin to experience the mountain towns that offer world-class outdoor recreation.

**Winter Park** holds an indelible spot in my heart; it's the place where, at the tender age of nine during a family vacation, I first strapped on skis and carved my "pizza path" down the snowy trails. It is also where my children first learned to ski as well.

Skiing is not the only first-time experience my family had at Winter Park. It is also where we shared exhilarating downhill mountain bike rides for the first time—a thrilling addition to any bucket list indeed.

It's quite the sight at *Winter Park*, watching mountain bikes hitch a ride on the back of ski lifts, only to descend the same hills with a rush of adrenaline. My kids and husband, seasoned BMX riders, excelled as they tore down the mountainsides. Meanwhile, I was the cautious one, gripping my bike tightly and shouting words of caution to my kids, hoping they wouldn't take a tumble as they soared off the rocks.

One unusual attraction *Winter Park* boasts is the largest alpine slide, offering a fast and fun ride down the mountain. But be careful—it can be hard to stop at the bottom! Steve almost got us kicked off when he bumped into the back of my cart.

Although my days of swooshing down the slopes may be behind me. Winter Park still delivers memorable experiences. During the writing of this book, I savored the best pretzel in the world at The **Noble Buck Brewing Co**. On a whim, I asked the waitress to surprise me with the finest light beer to complement their special, and I wasn't disappointed. [1]

This wasn't just any pretzel; it was a culinary masterpiece, presented hanging on a hook, and accompanied by a delectable dipping sauce. Having indulged in pretzels across the globe, I can confidently say this one stood out—an unexpected gastronomic highlight in the heart of the mountains.

As a child, I always honked the car horn when passing through the long **Eisenhower-Johnson Memorial Tunnel**, with the first tunnel opening in 1973 as part of the National Trails System—a network spanning all 50 states. Colorado's tunnel makes history as it cuts through a mountain and the *largest continental divide in the world*. The geologic crest runs through Colorado's Rocky Mountains, meaning that rivers on the west slope of the divide drain into the Pacific Ocean, while waters on the east slope drain into the Atlantic or Gulf of Mexico. Both sides of the mountain offer fun and adventure. Nestled within this alpine paradise are world-renowned resorts, each with their unique allure.

Colorado's majestic slopes beckon adventurers from around the globe, making them a premier destination for those passionate about mountainous activities. The state's crisp winter season typically starts in late October to mid-November and can last well into March, with snowfall varying each year. While early March might still see significant snow, by late March and April, the snowfall usually lessens. The thawing warmth begins to transform the pristine white canvas of the mountains. The area transitions from a winter wonderland to a summer playground.

***Keystone Resort***, conveniently located just a short drive from Denver, about 2.5 hours from DIA, is a haven for winter sports enthusiasts. Covering more than 3,000 acres and boasting 128 trails, it offers a fantastic experience for both skiers and snowboarders. The resort is celebrated for its dynamic culture and innovative terrain features, providing a diverse playground that caters to all levels of ability. Keystone regularly hosts events that highlight the vibrancy and creativity of the winter sports community, making it a top choice for those looking to enjoy the best of the Colorado Rockies.

The first time I experienced the thrill of **night skiing** was at the illustrious Keystone, a destination whose acclaim is well-earned, with its expansive reach across mountain peaks. Gliding down the slopes under the starlit sky brings a new dimension to the sport—a mix of exhilaration and ethereal solitude. The crisp night air and the quiet, with only the sound of your skis cutting through the crisp snow, create a magical experience that's worth braving the cold for. Another fun thing to do in the cold is **ice-skating** and was a hit with the kids.

However, the allure of a steaming hot tub at the end of a chilly run is undeniable, offering a soothing respite for tired muscles and a chance to unwind under the vast Colorado sky. Despite the enchanting appeal of night skiing, there's something special about being the first to carve tracks on the fresh morning slopes. The promise of untouched powder and the soft glow of dawn breaking over the mountains is a siren call for early risers, making those morning runs a perfect, pristine start to the day.

*Breckenridge* stands out as a ski destination that truly offers something for everyone. With its mix of challenging runs for seasoned skiers and gentler trails for families and beginners, it's a resort that caters to a diverse crowd. This versatility is further enhanced by the captivating charm of the adjacent mountain town, where visitors can stroll along historic Main Street, lined with quaint shops, cozy eateries, and lively bars.

**Vail Resort** offers over 5,000 acres of skiable terrain and is served by an impressive network of 34 lifts. It is among the world's most expansive ski destinations and holds the title of the second-largest single-mountain ski resort in North America. Vail is a place where the dreams of skiers and snowboarders come to life. Renowned for its expansive terrain, Vail provides an exceptional mountain experience. The resort is complemented by charming shops and diverse dining options for visitors to explore.

Fun Fact: Vail Resort is known for having the first-ever gondola, which dates back to December of 1962. Vail offers breathtaking views that can be enjoyed from this historic mountain town.[2]

Non-skiers can also experience the scenery, and children under 12 often ride free with a paying adult. Additionally, Vail Resort may offer food vouchers to guests who reach certain spending levels, so be sure to inquire about any current promotions during your visit.

*Aspen*, a name synonymous with luxury and exclusivity in the skiing world, boasts four distinct ski areas that grace the expanse of four magnificent mountains. Each area offers a unique, high-altitude experience that caters to a variety of preferences, whether you're seeking the thrill of challenging runs or the tranquility of a peaceful glide through powdery glades.

Aspen has hosted the *X-Games* for over 23 consecutive years, an event that has made it onto my bucket list. It looks like they have not yet signed the contracts for next year, but I hope it returns as this event is something I'm eager to see. It appears there was no fee to be in the park during the event, though I'm sure parking and getting up close will incur a high cost as the resort is known for being a high-end luxury destination.

## Southwestern Slope

Venturing into the North Central slopes of the Colorado Rockies is a haven of healing waters and mountain thrills. At **Steamboat Springs** you'll discover an all-season oasis nestled in the mountains. Steamboat is where the allure of natural hot springs and exceptional skiing converge. The hot springs, renowned for their therapeutic properties, provide a sanctuary for relaxation and rejuvenation, offering a perfect counterbalance to the adrenaline-fueled activities on the slopes.

Located just around a three-hour drive from *Denver International Airport (DIA),* the journey to Steamboat Springs is itself a scenic adventure, unveiling the rugged beauty of Colorado's landscape. For those looking for a quicker route, the **Yampa Valley Regional Airport (HDN)** is a mere 30-minute drive from the heart of *Steamboat Springs*, making access to this mountain retreat both convenient and swift.

World-class skiing and legendary hot springs have drawn visitors to *Steamboat Springs* for generations. Once there, skiers of all levels can appreciate the wide variety of beginner slopes that dot the mountain, ensuring that newcomers to the sport can learn and enjoy themselves in a comfortable and picturesque setting. Offering an emphasis on beginner and intermediate skiers, Steamboat is a great destination for both young and old. With its combination of soothing hot springs and abundant skiing opportunities, Steamboat Springs truly embodies the spirit of a Colorado getaway.

There are two main hot springs that are essential experiences for those looking to soak and relax in this mountain paradise, **Old Town Hot Springs** and **Strawberry Park Hot Springs**. In contrast, Old Town Hot Springs is situated right in the bustling downtown area of Steamboat Springs, providing a more accessible 102-103 degree for your soaking experience without sacrificing the benefits of the mineral waters. This facility boasts both indoor and outdoor pools, including expansive pool length, and is equipped with family-friendly water features such as a water slide and splash deck.

Strawberry Park Hot Springs is a rustic retreat about 5 miles from the heart of Steamboat Springs. Tucked away in a tranquil forested area, this natural haven features a series of stone-lined pools with temperatures ranging from a soothing 101 to a toasty 106 degrees Fahrenheit. *The Strawberry Park Hot Springs* pools are fed by the flow of mineral-rich hot springs, offering a still escape where you can unwind and enjoy the stunning vistas of the surrounding mountains and nature. *Strawberry Park Hot Springs* offers clothing optional after sundown until the next morning, therefore no children/minors are allowed after dark.[3]

Both hot springs offer distinctive atmospheres for visitors to decompress and heal. Whether you're seeking a rustic, intimate setting or a family-oriented aquatic center, Steamboat Springs' hot springs tradition is a must-do activity that perfectly complements the adventurous spirit of the Colorado Rockies.

Escape to the *Town of Festivals*, **Telluride** is a destination where the spirit of celebration meets outdoor adventure. The town hosts an array of events, including **The Telluride Bluegrass Festival** and **Telluride Jazz Festival** along with the **Telluride Film Festival.** It offers over *2,000 acres of skiable terrain* for winter sports enthusiasts. The area is also known for its culinary events such as *wine tastings* and *beer festivals.* With activities that cater to a wide range of interests, Telluride's skies and slopes are alive with excitement throughout the year. This resort takes a little longer to drive to than our previous destinations at around six hours from (DIA). Alternatively, you can arrive at **Telluride Regional Airport (TEX)**, which is approximately a 10-minute drive from the town center.

You can't forget the annual **Telluride Balloon Festivals**, with colorful balloons filling the gorgeous neon-blue mountain skies. The dates for this upcoming year haven't been posted yet, but usually, the festival takes place in July. You can also book a tour and soar through the mountains in a hot air balloon. Still on my bucket list.

Fun Fact: The historical link between Telluride and the legacy of **Nikola Tesla** is remarkable. Telluride was the site where **Tesla** engineered and constructed the world's first alternating current (AC) power plant.[4] This groundbreaking development revolutionized the way energy was distributed, enabling it to travel over much greater distances compared to direct current systems. In a twist of fate, the name Tesla is once again at the forefront of transformative change, this time spearheading the transition to electric vehicles, and continuing to shape the future of how we harness and utilize energy.

*Keep in mind that many of the high-country regions require chains or snow tires during the late months of November through early May. Additionally, be aware that Uber and Lyft drivers may not be permitted in all areas.*

## Colorado Mountain Towns
## Fun Things to Do in the Mountains

In nearly every ski town and larger mountain community, you can find a variety of activities such as four-wheeling, horseback riding, mountain biking, ATV tours, downhill and cross-country skiing.

Colorado is more than just its snow-clad slopes; it's a symphony of year-round festivities and activities, both indoors and out. Each ski destination, from the grand resorts to the quaint community hills, contributes a unique thread to the state's rich tapestry of skiing culture, offering endless opportunities for unforgettable winter adventures.

*Tip:*
*Renting is an affordable option. When you rent gear for skiing or biking you get a top-notch experience. They offer expensive, new bikes or skis, and snowboards, which give the chance to use the latest gear. Don't forget to put insurance on your equipment. If not, you risk paying a high premium should you damage anything.*

The grandeur of the *Eisenhower Tunnel* does not overshadow the smaller community ski areas scattered across the Colorado landscape. These charming spots offer a more intimate skiing experience, far from the bustle of larger resorts. With a warm, welcoming atmosphere, they are perfect for families, beginners, and those in search of a quieter day on the slopes. These hidden gems also boast shorter lift lines, lower costs, and the chance to ski like a local.

If you're seeking a shorter drive and a more budget-friendly option, **_Loveland & Eldora_** are smaller resorts just about an hour away from Denver. Both offer a great skiing experience at a more affordable price, though they are smaller and may not receive as much snow as the larger, higher-altitude resorts.

*Tip:*
*Remember sun protection! Sunglasses, sunscreen, and hats should be used even in the winter, you can get a sunburn at high altitudes.*

# CHAPTER 16

# HOLLYWOOD BACKDROP

## COLORADO'S CINEMATIC LANDSCAPES

Are you a movie buff? If so, Colorado is the place to check out. A tour of Colorado places used as movie sets would take you to almost every corner of the state. Outsiders often view Colorado as the "Wild West" so it makes sense that Colorado has been used as the backdrop to movies like *Butch Cassidy and the Sundance Kid* were filmed in the western state.[1] But Westerns are not the only films that have been shot in the Centennial State. The genres of movies filmed in Colorado range from comedies to action-packed thrillers.

I witnessed a spectacular sight one night back in 1990 while driving home from Denver. About halfway between Fort Collins and Denver, we crested the hill approaching the Longmont exit, greeted by an unexpected scene. Lights lit up the whole field. This location, along with the old Stapleton Airport, and the little church in the town of Mead served as the Hollywood setting for my favorite movie, the iconic film *Die Hard*.[2] They were recording the part of the snowmobile scene in the open field. You could see the lights of the set from many miles away.

It doesn't end there; comedy westerns, horror—what are you in the mood to watch? The towns of Aspen, Breckenridge, and even Estes Park have all served as backdrops for the big screen. *Dumb and Dumber* was filmed in various locations throughout Colorado, while *Indiana Jones and the Last Crusade* featured the desert train scene from the *Cumbres & Toltec Scenic Railroad* in Antonito. And let's not forget the famous *Stanley Hotel* in Estes Park that inspired *Stephen King's* horror classic, *The Shining*.

*Furious 7* was filmed at Pikes Peak. Even parts of *WarGames, Independence Day*, and *National Lampoon's Vacation* were filmed in Colorado. The list of movies filmed in this beautiful state is extensive and this is only a few. No matter what part of Colorado you visit, it's likely that Hollywood has also captured the view.

# CHAPTER 17

# BUC-EE'S

## WHERE ROADSIDE WHIMSY MEETS TEXAS-SIZED CONVENIENCE

The hoodie that my husband brought back from his Texas trip was a surprise. At first, I wasn't sure what to think about it - a pink hoodie with the **_Buc-ee's_** beaver logo on the top. Pink isn't my usual color choice; if it had been purple, that would have been a different story.

However, I wore it before the construction of the new Buc-ee's in Colorado, and every time, a stranger made an exciting comment. During the grand opening, the lines backed up I-25 for miles when Colorado's first *Buc-ee's* opened in March.

It was *tied for the largest in the country*, but three months later, a new location in Texas claimed that title.[1] It's not surprising they beat us by just *100 square feet*. It was fun to shop during the packed grand opening and see my first *Buc-ees's*.

So, what's special about this mega *116-pump gas station*? Although it looks like a truck stop, it's not.[2] In fact, they don't allow semi-trucks, which is part of the appeal to many. In many of my travel groups, bathrooms are a common topic of discussion. Are the bathrooms really as clean as everyone is talking about? I have to say yes, they are clean, and the door's close without cracks.

Many people have told me that the US is a weird country because most of the bathrooms have that long crack that you can see in and out of while you're doing your business. It was so nice to have my privacy in the cleanest gas station bathroom I have ever been in.

The pulled pork sandwich was reasonably priced and a quick grab-and-go option. I have also heard that their breakfast burritos are tasty. They have a wide variety of jerky and my dream, a fudge bar where you can even sample the fudge. It's a perfect stop for a quick rest if you are coming or going from Denver to the Loveland-Fort Collins area. We have filled up a couple of times there and have never had to wait for a pump.

This author would love to get her hands on a purple hoodie. Maybe someday I will see this book stocked on one of the end caps. My local photographer and I have even talked about how cool it would be to do a dual book signing there.

# CHAPTER 18

# NATURES UNEXPECTED NIGHTLIGHT

## NORTHERN LIGHTS

It has always been on my list to visit Alaska to see the ***Northern Lights***. I never imagined I would be able to witness the skies filled with color right here. After all my decades in Colorado, I couldn't have imagined in my wildest dreams that this would be a sight from our skies.

I went running about an hour or so after I started seeing posts about the bright aurora that was lighting up the skies. Nothing but darkness greeted me. Shout out to Jered at ***BridgemanPhotography*** for this breathtaking capture of these spectacular arrays of lights.[1]

What a shot! This celestial show honors our natural wonders while paying tribute to the hardworking spirit of those who tend our fields, run our trains, and keep our state moving forward from ranch to rail. This photo was taken near Carr on Hwy 85.

# CHAPTER 19

# LOVELAND COLORADO

## SWEETHEART CITY VALENTINE'S
## PARADISE 365 DAYS A YEAR

**N**estled north of Boulder and conveniently situated along I-25, ***Loveland, Colorado***, carries the endearing moniker of the *'Sweetheart City'* since its founding in 1877.[1] It has earned international acclaim for hosting the *Valentine Re-Mailing Program*, a heartwarming tradition that captivates the hearts of romantics world-wide. Each February, Loveland becomes the epicenter of affection as it receives over a hundred thousand Valentines.

These tokens of love are carefully enclosed in larger envelopes and delivered to Loveland, where volunteers inject them with a touch of magic by hand-stamping each with an exclusive Valentine's verse. Once adorned with this loving touch, the Valentines are sent forth to reach their final destinations, spreading love from the Sweetheart City to every corner of the planet.

As a Colorado native who resided in Loveland for several years, I have yet to experience the delight of receiving one of these hand-stamped Valentine's letters from the Loveland post office, despite the city's celebrated custom. Perhaps this year, I'll take matters into my own hands and send one to myself. After all, why wait for someone else to partake in such a sweet tradition?

You can see the love throughout the city with its unique heart sculptures. There's a small lake and a couple of parks in the middle of the city, including a sculpture park. Additionally, there are also lots of other lakes and campsites surrounding the town, perfect for outdoor enthusiasts.

***Boyd Lake***, located just outside of *Loveland*, is my favorite spot to kayak. We usually drop in right as we enter the park and paddle back to the secluded coves, where you can relax on the rocks or swim in the lake. Boyd is another great Colorado lake for boating and fishing.

Do you need to get some shopping therapy? Loveland has an extensive outdoor mall just off the interstate. ***The Promenade Shops at Centerra***, located on the east side of Interstate 25, boasts an impressive collection of 75 shops and restaurants as well as a ***MetroLux 14 Theatre***. This shopping haven is anchored by a main plaza, which serves as a community hub with its outdoor movies and events. Seasonally, the plaza trans-

forms into a winter wonderland with
an ice-skating rink, while year-round, visitors can enjoy leisurely strolls along the walking paths that lead to **Chapungu Sculpture Park**.

The west side of I-25 is home to a large outlet mall and several chain restaurants such as **In-N-Out Burger** and **Old Chicago**. If your significant other does not particularly enjoy shopping for clothing, books, and jewelry, I am sure they will enjoy spending some time at outdoor stores like **Sportsman's Warehouse** and **Scheels**. Note: there's a lot for kids to do at *Scheels* from a Ferris Wheel to arcade-type games and a play place. The outdoor and sporting mecca has a food court you can even walk under big fish tanks as you enter the store. Next to *Scheels*, there is also an impressive shooting range in **Liberty Firearms Institute** where customers are even able to rent and shoot a *Gatling Gun*.

Hockey fans, catch a hockey game and cheer on our minor league team, the **Colorado Eagles**. This photo was taken at the Budweiser Events Center (also known as the *Blue Arena*) during the playoffs, where I proudly wore my Colorado Avalanche jersey, supporting our NHL team, who were also in the

playoffs. You can attend comedy shows, basketball games, concerts, and other events at this venue, which is owned by Larimer County and located off I-25. Still on my bucket list is attending a major hockey game with the **Colorado Avalanche**. Exciting news: the *Colorado Eagles* will soon get a new arena in Greeley.

Driving towards the **Mariana Butte Golf Course** in Loveland, the breathtaking **Devil's Backbone** naturally commands your attention, presenting a dramatic backdrop as you approach the golf course. This striking geologic formation spans 3.5 square miles and 44,000 acres. Known as a "hogback", the Devil's Backbone is a result of sedimentary rock layers being thrust upward into undulating crests and then sculpted by erosion, leaving behind a prominent ridge of more resistant rock jutting out in stark relief against the sky.

Devil's Backbone open space has a lot to offer outdoor enthusiasts. If you enjoy hiking, biking, or horseback riding, *Devil's Backbone* provides a scenic destination to immerse yourself in the landscape. The open space offers picnic areas, restrooms, and drinking water (the water is turned off in the winter).

I have yet to experience a round of golf at *Mariana Butte*, but I have taken in the awe-inspiring view as I sipped a cold drink on the clubhouse porch. I've heard from Steve that there's a particular hole with a significant drop-off that poses a formidable challenge even to accomplished golfers. The distance is very deceiving due to the drop. Golf in Colorado is an absolute pleasure, with a diverse array of courses that satisfy any golfer's taste. From the urban greens to the quaint allure of mountain town fairways, there's something for everyone who wants to tee off in the Centennial State's stunning landscapes.

# CHAPTER 20

# THE BIG THOMPSON RIVER

## BEAUTY, RECREATION & RAW POWER

Venturing westward along Colorado Highway 34, the journey ascends into the majestic **Big Thompson Canyon**. This natural sanctuary is abundant with wonders, from the native trout swimming in its streams and river to the towering Ponderosa Pines, the untouched sagebrush landscapes, and the diverse wildlife that calls the canyon home.

Perfect for family excursions, all you need is a fishing rod, a camera to capture the memories, and a picnic to enjoy amidst the splendor of the parks nestled within the canyon. If you are on a leisurely drive or taking it slow so you can take in the scenery, it's customary to use the pull-offs to  allow faster drivers to pass you. The iconic landmark, **The Dam Store** is the first attraction as you enter the canyon. It is just outside of Loveland before you start the journey up the canyon through the mountains to Estes Park.

Looking for a delightful excursion that won't consume your entire day? The tower and family-owned gift shop experience have been charming visitors since 1969 and are worth a stop. This little treasure trove is brimming with curiosities and teasers that are sure to pique your interest. But the true allure lies just beyond the shop—step outside to an observation tower.

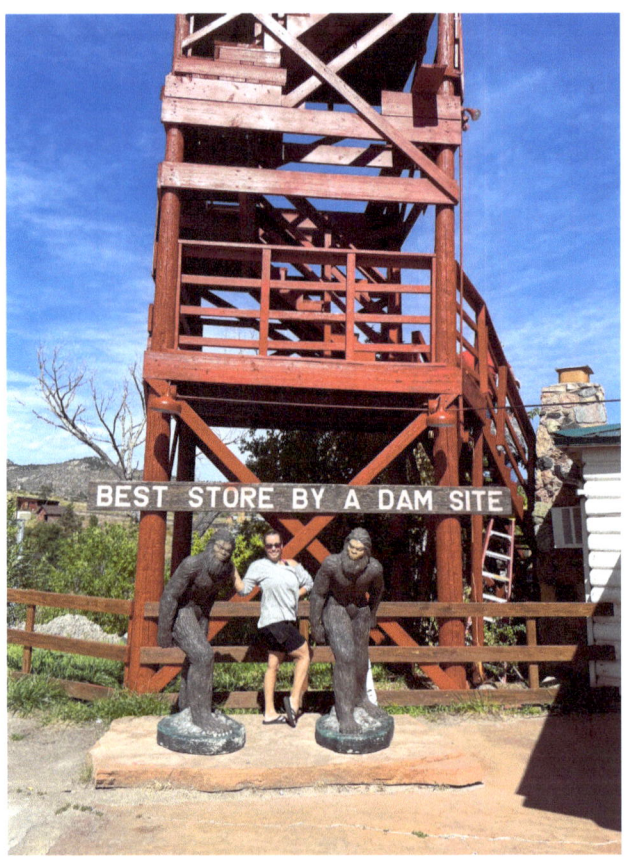

This local tower may only rise a few stories, yet the experience it offers is anything but small. The ascent is quick and manageable, making it an ideal activity for the whole family. Upon reaching the top, you are rewarded with panoramic views that afford a sense of being high above the ground. The landscape unfolds around you, inviting you to take in the beauty from this unique vantage point.

Looking to the west you can spot the dam, adding a touch of human ingenuity to the natural splendor. The sky stretches endlessly above, and the tranquility of the setting allows for a moment of reflection and appreciation for the world's expansive beauty.

Whether you're a local or a visitor, this quick climb up the stairs is an excellent way to enjoy the beauty of the area without dedicating an entire day. This stop is perfect for stretching your legs before the mountain drive and a free adventure with a rewarding payoff. It's an opportunity to enjoy stunning views, and even capture a whimsical photo with Bigfoot sculptures outside the shop.

The **Big Thompson River** is a force of nature that commands respect. Growing up, the river was a constant presence in my life, its power and potential for destruction were instilled in me through the stories my parents recounted during our scenic drives to Estes Park.

The river's history is marked by the devastating flood of 1976, which coincided with *Colorado's Centennial Celebrations*. The towns nestled at the top and bottom of the canyon were overwhelmed by the deluge, unable to contain the torrent of water that surged beyond the riverbanks.

The flood was swift, with heavy rains causing the river to swell rapidly. The signs along the river that urge people to climb to safety are not merely guidelines; they are life-saving advisories. The 1976 disaster claimed "*43 lives, many of whom were campers along the river, according to the USGS.*"[1] It also resulted in the loss of over 400 homes and more than 50 businesses, leaving a lasting imprint on the community.

Even decades later, the river's force was evident in the 2013 flood, which also took life. The sheer volume of rain and water during this event was a stark reminder of Mother Nature's unpredictable strength. When enjoying the scenic beauty of the Big Thompson, it's crucial to remain vigilant.

Riverbanks can be deceptive, transforming from peaceful to perilous in mere moments. Always prioritize safety when camping or engaging in recreational activities near these rivers to ensure that the power of nature is met with the respect and caution it deserves.

In the wake of the catastrophic 1976 flood, Larimer County took the opportunity to purchase several plots of land within the picturesque Big Thompson Canyon. Out of these acquisitions, four were transformed into County Parks, providing the public with access to the river for a variety of activities such as fishing, picnicking, and simply savoring the natural beauty of the canyon.

Open from April to October, the Big Thompson Parks welcome visitors from sunrise to sunset without charging an entrance fee. These serene escapes are conveniently situated along Highway 34, to the west of Loveland, Colorado, inviting everyone to immerse themselves in the tranquil splendor of the canyon.

The **Colorado Cherry Company** is a cherished stop on the journey through the canyon. The shop is a place where nostalgia and the simple pleasure of taste-testing collide. It's always amusing to hear my friends reminisce about their childhood visits, especially as we chuckle about the iconic *FREE SAMPLES* sign that beckons visitors from afar. Those trips are a shared piece of our past, where we, as wide-eyed kids, eagerly sampled the delicious cider alongside our parents.

Family-owned and operated to this day, the *Colorado Cherry Company* continues to delight with an array of beverages. For me, the standout is always their signature *Black Bing* and *Tart Red.* Colorado Cherry drinks are a refreshing testament to the state's bountiful orchards.

The experience doesn't end with the drinks, though. The pies are nothing short of phenomenal, each slice packed with flavor and a taste of home-baked goodness that's hard to find elsewhere.

The charm of the store extends beyond its edible offerings. The gift shop is a storehouse of locally crafted goods, including candles that fill the air with enchanting aromas and soaps that promise a sensory escape. It's the kind of place that captures the essence of Colorado's warm, inviting atmosphere.

Whether you're on the classic route to Estes Park or taking the scenic drive from Boulder up to Lyons, the Colorado Cherry Company awaits, ready to enchant you with its sweet offerings and local charm.

# CHAPTER 21

# ESTES PARK

## THE QUAINT TOWN EVEN LOCALS CAN'T RESIST

I f you are looking for activities, you are in for a treat at **Estes Park**. A short drive west from the Fort Collins/Loveland area is a quaint little town nestled in the Western Slope of the Rocky Mountains. There are plenty of things to choose from. Here are some of my favorite vacation activities to enjoy.

The most common mode of transportation to the area is by car, offering flexibility and the opportunity to enjoy the scenic route at your own pace. Additionally, for those arriving at Denver International Airport, there are shuttle services available that provide convenient access to the destination. These shuttles are a hassle-free alternative, especially for those who prefer not to drive or want to avoid the responsibility and cost of car rental.

If you are driving to Estes Park, there are several routes you can take, but the most direct route is via US-36 W. This route takes you through Boulder and into the town of Estes Park. The drive is picturesque, and you will pass through several small towns along the way. You can also head up from Loveland via U.S. Route 34.

*Tip:*

*Given the winding nature of the roads, it's not uncommon for travelers to experience motion sickness. It's always a good idea to come prepared with a bag handy, just in case someone feels unwell during the drive. You may also want to pick up some Dramamine at the pharmacy. These precautions can help ensure a more comfortable journey for all passengers.*

If you prefer not to drive, there are several **Shuttle Services** available from Denver and other front-range cities. These shuttles will take you directly to Estes Park; some even offer door-to-door service. The cost of the shuttle varies depending on the service, but it is generally more affordable than renting a car.

You can get an ***Uber*** or ***Lyft*** at the airport to take you to the mountain town. However, getting back might be a problem! There are very few drivers around the little town, and many from the front-range cities don't want to run up the mountain to pick people up.

Once you arrive in Estes Park, getting around is easy. The town is small and walkable; however, it is a mountain town, so the air is thin and there are hills. There are several parking lots available if you choose to drive.

*Tip:*
*There is a little trolley bus and other shuttles in the town. Keep in mind that some of the lodgings, like hotels and cabins, are on the outskirts of town, and might not be within walking distance or on the shuttle services routes.*

Incredible trails can be found around the park. As an avid hiker, I recommend checking out the ***Bear Lake Trailhead***, which offers a variety of trails for all skill levels. The ***Emerald Lake Trail*** is a personal favorite of mine, with stunning views of the Rocky Mountains and a picturesque lake at the end of the trail. Don't forget to bring plenty of water and snacks, and always be prepared for changing weather conditions.

If you are looking for a more relaxed activity, Estes Park has plenty of picnic areas to enjoy a meal with family and friends. The ***Lily Lake***

**Picnic Area** is a popular spot, with stunning views of the surrounding mountains and a peaceful lake to enjoy. Pack a picnic basket with your favorite snacks and drinks and take in the natural beauty of the park.

Estes Park is also a great destination for fishing enthusiasts. The *Big Thompson River* is a popular spot for *fly fishing*, with plenty of trout to catch. You can also check out **Lake Estes**, which offers a variety of fish species. I have fished there many times and have yet to bring in a catch. Over the years, others have told me that there are fish in the lake, but I'm not quite sure if I believe them. Before you go, make sure to get a fishing license and follow all regulations to protect the environment and wildlife.

This small town is home to a variety of wildlife, including elk, bighorn sheep, and black bears. If you are interested in wildlife watching, I recommend checking out the **Rocky Mountain National Parks Visitor Centers** which offer historical exhibits with interpretive information about the park and the wildlife that call it home. You can also take a scenic drive through the park and keep an eye out for wildlife along the way.[1]

A round of golf at the local courses is a one-of-a-kind experience, often involving dodging elk that like to graze on the manicured greens. Lake **Estes Park-18** offers a picturesque course, ideal for a longer round, while **Lake Estes-9** is a charming green that has been the setting for countless memorable tournaments for Steve and his father, often proving to be a favorite spot for them.

Moose were re-introduced to the Rocky Mountains by wildlife experts in 1978. Over the years, their population has grown and they have migrated throughout the Colorado Rockies. These beautiful creatures have been spotted in the town of Estes Park and surrounding areas. We've been advised that the swampy areas of Rocky Mountain National Park are prime spots for sightings. Steve admires them for their dual nature—peaceful by default but fiercely protective when threatened or if their young are involved.

Although Steve and I have visited Estes Park recently, we have not been able to spot one of these massive mammals on our visits. As we explore the lush landscapes of the national forest, we remain hopeful of encountering these guardians of nature, a testament to the wild heart of the park.

Autumn brings out the majestic bugling ***Rocky Mountain Elk***. As the streets and parks of Estes Park come alive with the sound of nature's call, the sight of bulls swarming is a spectacle to behold. With a deep, resonant bugle, these magnificent elk make their presence known, calling out to potential mates during the breeding season.

The males will challenge each other for dominance smashing their antlers together, but be aware, and stay far away from these mighty creatures. Many people have been injured or killed for getting too close, especially during the elk rut. This incredible display, a mix of raw animal instinct and majestic beauty, is a phenomenon that draws visitors from near and far. Witnessing the elk's bugling is a unique experience, particularly from mid-September through October, and sometimes even as late as November. It's a seasonal ritual that embodies the wild spirit of Estes Park and one of the many wonders of the natural world.

When visiting the park, there are many lodging options from cabins to hotels, and even a *YMCA*. I can still remember Steve and I attending a marriage retreat in our early 30s. The grounds look much the same today and it is an affordable place to stay with activities on site.

If you're looking for a more rustic camping experience. The nearby *Rocky Mountain National Park* offers several campgrounds, including **Moraine Park Campground** and **Glacier Basin Campground**. There are also a couple of **KOA** *campgrounds*. These campgrounds offer stunning views of the mountains and easy access to hiking trails and other outdoor activities.

If you're looking for a more luxurious camping experience, there are many cabin and glamping style options around. Little cabins that are complete with comfortable beds, heaters, and private bathrooms.

Are you a fan of the paranormal? The **Stanley Hotel's** haunted reputation will not disappoint. Take a ghost tour or book a room in the infamous Room 217, where *Stephen King* wrote his novel *The Shining*. To this day, it still falls in my top 5 scariest horror movies. That darn tricycle scared the hell out of me.

The *Stanley Hotel* presents a spectrum of accommodations to cater to various tastes and budgets, from the understated elegance of classic rooms to the indulgent luxury of its suites. Each guest room is a unique fusion of modern amenities set against the backdrop of the hotel's historic charm. While amenities vary by room, many include flat-screen TVs and coffee makers, ensuring a comfortable and convenient stay.

For those captivated by the allure of the *Stanley's* otherworldly reputation, haunted rooms are available for booking. These rooms, legendary for their paranormal visitors, offer an experience unlike any other. Guests staying in these rooms have the opportunity to delve into the hotel's haunted history, accompanied by a ghost tour and special amenities to set the mood for a thrilling encounter.

Whether you're drawn to the comfort of a classic room or the allure of a haunted adventure, this hotel accommodates both, enhanced by the stunning scenery of the surrounding mountains and promising a memorable experience in the heart of the Colorado Rockies.

Inside the *Stanley Hotel*, the **Whiskey Bar & Lounge** offers the perfect ambiance for relaxation and indulgence in a drink. With a vast array of whiskeys from around the world, aficionados and newcomers alike will find something to delight their palate. The bar also features a selection of creative cocktails and casual fare, ensuring a satisfying experience for all who visit. Whether you're there to enjoy a classic dram or to explore new flavors, the *Whiskey Bar & Lounge* is a haven for those who appreciate the finer spirits in life.

Adding to the hotel's enchantment, my sister chose this picturesque venue and **The Music Room** for her wedding. It was, without a doubt, the most beautiful ceremony I have ever attended. The Stanley Hotel's grandeur, combined with the breathtaking backdrop of the *Colorado Rockies*, created a fairy-tale setting for her special day. My favorite photograph is the one where she and my parents are standing with the grand piano elegantly poised in the background. It captures a moment of grace and adds a touch of classical charm to the memory.

The experience was not only a testament to the hotel's historic elegance but also to its capacity to host events that are as majestic as its surroundings.

*The word on the street is that the property is being sold. It will be fascinating to see what becomes of this historical landmark with the hotel changing ownership.*

# CHAPTER 22

# STANDING ON TOP OF THE WORLD

## A JOURNEY TO CONQUER THE MOUNTAIN

The **Rocky Mountain National Park** is a must-visit destination, boasting an expansive terrain of forests, mountains, and diverse wildlife.[1] Visitors can engage in activities like hiking, rock climbing, or simply soaking in the breathtaking vistas. Additionally, there are professional guided tours available, guaranteeing that none of the park's significant landmarks go unseen.

Rocky Mountain National Park boasts 450 miles of rivers and streams, along with 156 lakes, creating a rich ecosystem for wildlife such as moose, bighorn sheep, deer, and elk. Bird enthusiasts will find it a paradise for observing a variety of species in their natural habitat. For those interested in camping and fishing, the park provides ample opportunities, though it's worth noting that only 48 of the lakes are stocked with Colorado's renowned trout.

I highly recommend a drive up the highest continuous paved road in the United States, **Trail Ridge Road**. From there, you can experience the feeling of being on top of the world without having to hike to get there. Keep in mind this road is closed during the winter due to deep snow.

The drive will take you across the **_Continental Divide_** at 12,183 feet above sea level, but be sure to read the signs carefully, as some roads are one-way and impossible to turn around on.

For a memorable adventure, book a tour that takes you to the top of the summit in a truck with open-air benches. Given the park's high elevation, staying hydrated is crucial to help prevent altitude sickness, and even in summer months jackets are advised.

This is one of my favorite pictures that my daughter took on my 48th birthday drive. It captures the love I have for this state and its picturesque scenery, as well as the passion I have for this man, who has traveled the world with me. Thanks for being my travel buddy and the love of my life.

What does it take to "stand on top of the world?" I'm about to be brutally honest about what it's like to take on a Colorado mountain. These majestic peaks are no laughing matter!

***Longs Peak***, the tallest mountain in Rocky Mountain National Park and one of Colorado's 15 highest summits, towering at 14,259 feet marking my first fourteener.[2] While it's not the tallest mountain in the world—an accolade that belongs to Mount Everest at 29,032 feet, a peak that takes most climbers 7-9 weeks to ascend with limited time in the "death zone"—climbing Everest isn't on my agenda. However, like Everest, Longs Peak commands respect.

We all need oxygen. As a Colorado native, I can attest that this state adores the great outdoors, and even we locals train before tackling these high elevations. Colorado isn't nicknamed the Mile High State because of marijuana—though that's also accessible here—but because Denver sits a mile above sea level. Visitors from sea level are already at a disadvantage: the higher you climb, the less oxygen there is, between 17-25% less, which significantly impacts the risk of altitude sickness and how our brains and bodies function.

As a child, I watched my grandparents from Kansas struggle to breathe when they visited us. I've even seen many Colorado natives fall ill in the national park, simply from driving through the thin air, long before any hiking begins.

## Training for the Climb

A group of 30 of us trained for six months, but only 13 reached the summit. For a half year, I focused on getting into shape for this endeavor. I named it my summit challenge. My objective was to reach the peak of the 15-mile mountain hike. Here's a snapshot of the vision board and training routine that steered my preparations:

**Vision Board**: Visualizing the dream and outlining the path to the top is essential. I created a large poster board adorned with photos and maps of *Longs Peak*, which I displayed with pride. A monthly flip calendar, along with a box of stickers, marked the completion of each day's workout, and proper meal intake. This kept me focused on the reward of witnessing ***Mills Glacier,*** which is vanishing due to global warming, and ultimately the summit. None of my family members nor most of my instructors had ever completed the hike to the very summit.

**Endurance Walking:** It was crucial to be able to walk 22 miles in a single day. The logic was simple, if I couldn't walk this much managing a hike with this many miles had no chance of success, especially with thinner air at higher altitudes. The extra seven miles were for building endurance to account for the incline and preparing for any potential emergencies. Starting with achievable goals, I aimed to walk a mile and a half each morning and evening, gradually increasing my distance every day.

**Nutrition: Diet:** A healthy and nutritious diet is key. It's important to remember that any diet should provide sufficient protein and vitamins to support the intense training and ultimately the calorie-burning hike.

**Cardiovascular Fitness:** Once I built some endurance, my trainer had me constantly walking and running. Despite my aversion to running, it was essential for strengthening my lungs and ankles while building stamina. I started with a quarter-mile and worked up to at least 10 miles by the three-month mark.

**Local Trail Hikes**: During the summer break, I tackled as many local trails as possible. The bigger the hills, the better it was for training.

**Pack Preparation**: I practiced carrying a fully loaded day pack, including multiple water bottles and all necessary gear. It's vital to be self-sufficient, as no one else will carry your equipment. I chose a comfortable backpack with a hydration system, allowing hands-free drinking would be essential for the hike. Water weighs over 8lbs per gallon so preparing my body to carry the weight was essential.

**Day of the Hike:** We started at 2:00 am with a hearty breakfast, followed by last-minute bathroom breaks and hydration checks at 2:30 am. Ensuring everyone had plenty of water was crucial for preventing altitude sickness and dehydration.

**12–15-Hour Day:** Our group had a 2:45 am departure time. Depending on how fast you hike you can expect a 12–15-hour day. Being an amateur with short legs, it was clear in the very beginning that it was going to take the upper amount of time. The goal was to be back before sunset/dinner time around 5:30. It's easier to hike in the morning when your body is rested. Trying to make it down the mountain when you are exhausted and in the dark is dangerous.

**Physical Maps:** Having physical maps is indeed essential. Knowing how to read a map and use a compass is a fundamental skill for any hiker venturing into remote areas.

Our physical maps had been marked with resting points and times that we were expected to hit checkpoints. We all have our wonderful phones, and a good tracking GPS is a great thing to throw in your pack. However, these devices can run out of power, malfunction, or lose signal.

I also packed a compass just in case we got lost. I carried two maps in my bag, one was of the park trails that outlined the walking path and one of the National Park. My family had been told where and when I would be hiking. I would be checking back in with a designated contact person after we returned to base camp.

## Left Behind

No one left behind was the goal. If someone had to stop, they needed a buddy. Both people would wait at the marked trail until the rest of the group picked them up on the way back down.

I don't want to scare anyone away from taking this incredible adventure; however, the reality is the mountains are home to bears, mountain lions, and rattlesnakes. Aside from the wildlife, at 11,500 feet we will hit the tree line where exposure to the elements becomes a real danger. Being prepared and with a buddy will help keep us safe.

Hitting the tree line is a strange feeling. It's cold and even the moisture changes standing this high. I remember our guide saying it's okay to stop; even the pine trees, aspen, and most animals can't survive at this altitude due to lack of oxygen. Lightheadedness and altitude sickness took down half of the people who made it to this point. Two more dropped out less than a mile later. Even during the short breaks, I found myself not wanting to stop for too long of a break or my muscles would start to ache and cramp. On the other hand, too many steps would leave you out of breath.

Hands-free water and easy foods to eat as you walk are essential. Easy-to-pack items like oranges and apples make great snacks. The PB&J would be eaten at the top during the brief lunch break. Since the goal was to be back before dark our lunch stop was very short.

After six months, at the age of 12, I was among the handful of kids standing at the top of the Colorado Rocky Mountains. Thank you to my teachers who put up with all of us, and the gym coaches who made us run a mile every Monday, Wednesday, and Friday. I might have been the slowest kid in class, but I made it to the top of the mountain, leaving many of the faster kids miles behind.

### Thank You

To my parents who worked extra hours for my camp fees and bought the cool star stickers that filled the *focus board, thank you. A big shout-out to the Eco Week* staff, parents, and teachers who took us all under their wings. Through your time and teaching, you helped open my world to travel.

Since that day, I have done what we talked about at the top of the summit. Recently I hiked to the tops of Costa Rica's jungles to overlook Nicaragua's volcanoes. My teacher was correct, it's breathtaking. A year later, I would stand atop one of those volcanoes with my youngest daughter. All these hikes were challenging, but none would have been possible without training and the big dream of standing on top of the world.

### Packing list & Navigation tools

**Walking Stick**: A good walking stick was a must. You can purchase a telescopic one that is lightweight, however; we found many branches along the trails that met our needs. Just be sure to grab yours before you reach the tree line.

**Maps, Compass, and GPS:** Knowing how to use and read them is priceless.

**Whistle:** A whistle is a crucial piece of safety equipment that every hiker should carry. It serves as a reliable tool for signaling when you need help. If you're hiking with children, it's important to give them the opportunity to practice using the whistle before you hit the trails. This isn't just a novelty; it's a precaution. Allow them to familiarize themselves with the whistle at home, so they understand it's not a toy. In the wilderness, the sound of a whistle is a signal for an emergency, and its piercing call is designed to alert other hikers and rangers to your location. Make sure everyone in your hiking party knows that the whistle should only be used in genuine situations of distress.

**Sun protection:** (sunglasses, sunscreen, hat) As previously mentioned hiking in Colorado is at a high altitude and as such is closer to the sun. I highly recommend protecting yourself as sunburns can ruin a great day of hiking.

**Insulation/Extra Clothing**: I favor cargo pants with zip-off legs. They allow you to reattach the lower sections when it gets cold. I also recommend having leggings or long-johns, as the temperature fluctuates frequently and the weather in the mountains is always changing. Many layers of clothing allow you to adjust as the weather changes during the day.

**Illumination/Flashlight**: I prefer headlamps as they keep my hands free. It's wise to start with new batteries and carry an extra set just in case.

**First Aid**: Pack a small first aid kit with emergency essentials and a lot of bandages. On the longer hikes, everyone had blisters on their feet.

**Snake Bite Kit**: Colorado is home to rattlesnakes, and a bite can happen suddenly and without warning. It's crucial to be prepared with a snake bite kit and to familiarize yourself with its use before setting out on your hike.

**Good hiking shoes:** Make sure that the shoes are broken in. Many hikers bring two pairs. This allows you to change out if your footwear gets wet or is uncomfortable.

**Extra Socks**: Always pack an extra pair. Carrying extra socks is not only essential for keeping your feet dry and warm in case they get wet or cold, but they also have a range of versatile uses in an emergency. Socks can serve as makeshift tourniquets, bandages, or slings. They can be tied together to help construct a shelter by securing branches or even used as gloves to keep your hands warm. I always pack a couple of extra pairs of good-quality wool socks—they're excellent for insulation and keeping your feet comfortable, no matter the conditions.

**Fire:** In the event you are not able to make it back to camp you will need to make a fire. Waterproof matches, a lighter, or a fire starter are a must.

**Nutrition:** Pack extra food. You are going to burn a lot of calories and may need some extra should an unexpected event happen. Remember, there are no convenience stores in the wilderness.

**Hydration:** Bring extra water! I recommend a *CamelBak* that fits in a comfortable backpack or a hydration system that has a pack. Being able to drink hands-free, especially on the day of the hike is important. It's recommended to take at least 3-4 liters of water. Depending on your pack size that's a little over one full water bladder. Water is heavy; however, I wish I had taken 3 bladders. The upside is the pack gets lighter the more you drink and once again staying hydrated is key. But remember to save some for the way down too.

**Hydration Plus**: When venturing out on a hike, it's not just water that you need—it's essential to maintain your electrolyte balance too. Electrolyte hydration packs are a must-have for me and my outdoor enthusiast. They go beyond the hydration provided by water alone, replenishing the vital minerals and salts that your body loses through sweat. Symptoms of dehydration, such as lightheadedness, can escalate quickly, but with these specialized liquid packs, you can drink fluids enriched with electrolytes to help prevent such issues. They're a convenient and efficient way to keep your body's hydration and electrolyte levels in check, especially during strenuous activity. So, before you hit the trail, make sure you're prepared with an electrolyte hydration pack. It could be a crucial step in safeguarding your health and ensuring a successful hike.

**LifeStraw:** A *LifeStraw* is a small straw that filters the water so you can drink from the lakes and rivers in an emergency.

**Emergency Shelter**: You can do a lot with a space blanket, plus they are small and compact. (tent, bivy sack, space blanket)

**Compact Rain Jackets:** It's always smart to have a rain jacket on hand for those unexpected downpours. You can find compact, disposable ones that are easy to toss into your pack. Steve and I prefer the foldable, pocket-sized rain jackets. They may be a bit larger than plastic throwaways, but they provide superior warmth and protection from the elements, making them well worth the extra space in our hiking kit.

**Heavy Jacket:** It's cold at the top of the world! I love layering my warm hoodie under my rain jacket. However, during the late and early spring, having a heavy coat that is packable isn't a bad idea.

# CHAPTER 23

# LAKES - CAMPING - HUNTING & FISHING

## A SPORTSMAN'S DREAM DESTINATION

With over *4,000 lakes*, more than *3,900 state park camping spots*, and countless other locations outside of the parks, Colorado is a prime destination for camping, hunting, fishing, and simply relaxing by the fire. And that's just the beginning.

The hunt is on. Hunting is a popular activity for many in Colorado, where the emphasis is always on safety, especially during hunting season when parks are often filled with hunters. Securing a chance to hunt deer is still on my bucket list, as it requires *drawing a limited deer tag* in Colorado. At this time hunters can just pay for an elk tag. Today rates on bull and cow elk are $62.72 for residents, out-of-state hunters are looking at about $761. Hunters are responsible for packing out their kill, which can be quite a challenge.

Friends of mine who hunt have found success in places like **Lory State Park, Steamboat Springs,** and **Roosevelt National Forest**, to name just a few. It's important to remember that not all state parks permit hunting; *Rocky Mountain National Park* is one such place where hunting is *NOT Allowed*.[1]

Colorado boasts a rich avian population, with the Lark Bunting honored as our state bird. Enthusiasts may also spot majestic creatures such as the Golden Eagle or Bald Eagle, as well as woodpeckers, Blue

Jays, and various species of ducks. The state offers a diverse array of birds for both watching and hunting. According to the official Colorado state list, as of *February 2022, there are 514 recognized bird species.*

*Tip:*
*Colorado has Poison Ivy, the saying we grew up with was "Leaves of three, let it be!".*

If hunting isn't your thing, you can find several places to camp throughout this Rocky Mountain state. **Lake Granby**, with a depth of *221 feet and spanning 7,000 acres*, is renowned not only for its size and beauty but also for the memorable camping experiences it offers, such as the unforgettable trip taken by the Page family.[2]

The Pages' adventure started with the pitching of our large family tent, a routine setup that typically promised comfort despite the frequent mountain rains. We were well-prepared, with a rain mat under the tent and a collection of card games to pass the time while nestled inside our shelter. With numerous kids in tow, our backpacks, and sleeping bags were neatly arranged on the tent floor, poised for the nights ahead.

However, the skies had other plans. The rain, an anticipated guest, overstayed its welcome, pouring down incessantly. My family's spirits remained high at first, but as the rain continued, the camping pad began to flood. The relentless downpour turned our shelter into a soggy haven, and warmth became a distant memory as the days went on.

Caught in a relentless deluge, the Pages watched as Lake Granby's potential for fishing and boating adventures slipped away with each raindrop. Our camping story became one of nature's unpredictability, a reminder that even the most meticulous plans can be undone by the relentless elements. Yet, despite the dampened fabric of the tent, clothes, and sleeping bags, Lake Granby's maintained its majestic allure, standing as a testament to the wild and untamed beauty of Colorado's great outdoors.

Another popular body of water is **Grand Lake.** Spanning more than 500 acres with depths plunging to 389 feet, Grand Lake embodies its own grandeur as Colorado's largest and deepest natural lake.[3] It's a sight I've witnessed and terrain I've hiked around, yet it remains an unchecked item on my summer bucket list. One day, I aspire to float my kayak on its waters and attempt to cross its breadth.

My favorite fishing spot is more than just a place to cast a line, it's a repository of cherished family memories. ***Red Feather Lakes*** have been our go-to spot to get our outdoor fix. [4]

Our family has always loved camping, and every trip included attempts at fishing. When I was younger, my dad would humorously claim that there were no fish in Colorado, as our efforts with different baits and spots, and the long hours holding our poles, often seemed in vain. Those long fishing days with my dad are among my fondest memories.

Echoing my childhood, my children also spent many hours by the water with scant results. Although there is a fee to stay in Red Feather parks, some of the best spots for camping are outside the park's boundaries in the 612,000-acre *Roosevelt National Forest* that surrounds it.[5] If you decide to camp outside of *Red Feather Park* you can purchase a day pass for parking at the lake.

Despite our historically modest success, we kept returning because of the exceptional campsites. However, our luck turned one year at *Red Feather Lakes.* Our persistence paid off spectacularly on a Father's Day outing. After years of trying, we started catching fish right and left. This success has continued over the years, as my family consistently makes great catches of *Rainbow Trout* at **Dowdy**, the largest of the Red Feather Lakes.[6] There are 12 named lakes in the area; however, many of them are private. The public lakes are well-stocked, which likely contributes to our fruitful expeditions.

When you plan a fishing or hunting trip in Colorado, it's crucial to remember to secure a license. Park rangers are often on patrol, and the fine for fishing and hunting without a license can be exorbitantly expensive. Obtaining a license is not only a legal requirement but also supports the conservation efforts that maintain our fishing spots for future generations. So, ensure you're prepared: get your license, find your ideal spot, and perhaps you'll stumble upon your family's new favorite fishing destination.

At the risk of being disowned by my father-in-law for telling you about his favorite fishing hole, another great spot is **Bellaire Lake Campground.**[7] Situated in the picturesque and sought-after Red Feather Lakes area, *Bellaire* offers easy access to the lake through a *wheelchair-accessible boardwalk* just a short distance away. The surrounding landscape is dotted with distinctive rock formations and provides stunning mountain vistas. Anglers can enjoy fishing at *Bellaire Lake*. Each campsite is equipped with a tent pad, a fire grate, and a picnic table, and for added safety, campsites featuring a tent pad also include a bear locker. Visitors can choose from single, double, or triple sites, with some offering the convenience of electrical hookups for those that enjoy "glamping".

These are just a few of my favorites among the many beautiful lakes and camping spots scattered throughout the mile-high state. There's something to be said about the rustic charm of tent camping, and I've certainly done my share of it. Reflecting on the past, I sometimes wish we had splurged on an RV/Camper when the kids were young. Raising four children was costly, so we made do with tents and poles. It took a couple of years to save up for our gently used pop-up camper. Camping was almost an every weekend affair, and I found myself dreading the discomfort of sleeping on the ground and the lack of private bathroom facilities, always dreaming of the day we would own a home on wheels.

It wasn't until our late forties that we were able to check that dream off our list. If you're considering RV or camper life, there are a few things you should know. Not all national parks accommodate them, and the roads can be narrow, winding, steep, and fraught with tight turns. When you do stay at a campground, it's important to be considerate of others' space. Always walk around their sites to reach your destination; like you, they've paid for their little slice of the outdoors.

For those who don't own a truck or camper, there are options such as renting one that's already set up through various platforms like *VRBO, Airbnb,* and even some websites dedicated to outdoor stays. Many *KOAs* also offer rental availability.

One of the joys of camping is the ability to cook outside. Cooking outside somehow makes the food taste even better. Make sure to watch signs and research the area you are staying in. During the dry seasons many locations have high fire risks and having open campfires may not be allowed. One of the benefits of an RV is that with many models you can cook outside during fire bans.

Check out the packing list in the chapter *Standing on Top of the World.* This list also includes my must-haves for camping. Tip: I also added a campfire coffee pot. A morning cup of coffee during the sunrise just makes camping that much better.

**Bonus Spot:**

Near Red Feather, you'll find the distinctive ***Drala Mountain Center***, a Buddhist sanctuary offering meditation sessions, educational workshops, and reflective conferences.[8]

This tranquil retreat is also the site of the largest stupa in North America. Standing at an impressive 108 feet, this temple-like edifice is an emblem of the quest for peace, harmony, and balance for all beings and welcomes visitors from all spiritual backgrounds to appreciate its grandeur and significance.

# CHAPTER 24

# MAKE YOUR TASTE BUDS DANCE

## COLORADO THROUGH THE EYES OF A LOCAL

I find the harvest season in Colorado to be a time of pure delight for the taste buds. The fresh foods of Colorado begin to showcase their goodness early in the season, as street-side tents start popping up around the towns. You can find all kinds of fresh produce; for instance, rhubarb season runs from May to early July, while the watermelon and cantaloupe harvest spans from August through October.

From late June to early October, the state transforms into a paradise for fresh produce enthusiasts. The appearance of ***Palisade Peaches*** stands on street corners is a highlight, marking the availability of these succulent fruits. Anyone in Colorado during this period should make it a point to stop by a tent—the delectable peaches are simply unforgettable. You can even visit the town Palisade, about a four-hour drive from Denver 233 miles.

The cherry harvest, which runs from late June to late July, is just as delightful. **Cherries** are among my personal favorites, yet Colorado is home to a diverse range of growers, from expansive orchards to small family farms. I've never been disappointed by any stand during the harvest season. For those mindful of their spending, remember that you can often buy fruit in any quantity, and prices can vary between vendors.

From July to mid-October, you will find fresh **roasted peppers** available. From hot to mild, they will roast them for you while you wait. Then there's the **sweet corn**—just thinking about it makes my mouth water. The anticipation starts with the planting season, and although I must be patient, the wait is always rewarded. Sweet corn is a staple at Colorado cookouts, and local farmers never fail to impress with their crop's quality. I particularly love it when the corn is in the botanical fruit stage, with kernels that are tender, milky, and bursting with sweetness.

August brings in the world-famous ***Rocky Ford Watermelons***.[1] My taste buds are just dancing thinking about the juicy, farm-grown fruit. There's truly nothing that compares to the experience of enjoying farm-fresh foods from Colorado. Take the opportunity to visit a local farmer's tent and treat yourself to the state's bounty of delicious, flavor-packed produce that's sure to make your taste buds sing. Whether it's fruits, vegetables, or other artisanal treats, Colorado's fresh fare is not to be missed.

## Celebration of Colorado
## Autumn Adventure with a Twist October Festivities

October is a time of celebration across many parts of the world, and Colorado is no exception. It's a season that marks the end of the harvest and the beginning of preparations for the upcoming winter. Throughout the state, you can find an array of festivals in nearly every town, each with its unique flavor and charm.

Each Labor Day weekend, Denver hosts ***A Taste of Colorado***, an event many consider the official farewell to summer. This celebration is echoed in many mountain towns, which also present their own versions of *A Taste of Colorado*. Festival-goers can enjoy a full day of live music, an assortment of arts and crafts booths, a diverse selection of food trucks, and a fun-filled kids' area.

The culinary scene is a dream state: mouthwatering, taste bud-popping, sweet to savory, farm-to-table, homemade to outdoor cook-ing, festival foods to fine dining at top resorts, small mountain picnics, and locally-owned restaurants and breweries—Colorado has once again proven itself to be a world-class destination.

***Corn mazes*** in Colorado make an autumn adventure with a twist. In the farming regions of Colorado, corn mazes become a hallmark of the fall season. These intricate labyrinths offer a delightful way to enjoy the crisp autumn air and the rustic charm of the countryside. While navigating through one of the haunted mazes, you can savor the taste of fresh corn on the cob, a seasonal treat that pairs wonderfully with the playful challenge of finding your way out.

To complement the experience, indulge in a cup of hot chocolate or apple cider—both are perfect for keeping warm during these outings. And if you're venturing into the higher country, you might even be greeted by a gentle dusting of snow, adding a touch of winter's magic to the autumnal fun. Whether you're there for the thrills of the haunted maze or simply to enjoy the seasonal offerings, corn mazes in Colorado provide a picturesque setting for creating lasting memories.

## CHAPTER 25

# FALL FOLIAGE

## A SYMPHONY OF AUTUMN HUES

There's an indescribable charm to the crispness of the autumn breeze, the symphony of leaves crunching beneath your feet, and the captivating mountain vistas. It's a period for contemplation, a chance to savor the wonders of the natural world, and an opportunity to create lasting memories. Autumn in Colorado is a season of enchantment when the mountains are set aflame with a spectacular display of colors. There's no better way to immerse oneself in the splendor of fall than by embarking on a scenic mountain drive.

Each year, to celebrate my birthday, Steve orchestrates a special mountain excursion to revel in the autumnal beauty. We navigate the winding scenic byways, pausing at various overlooks to absorb the awe-inspiring vistas of golden aspens, the fiery hues of red, and the vivid oranges painting the landscape.

The prime time to experience Colorado's fall foliage typically falls between September and October. However, the precise timing of peak colors is influenced by factors such as specific location, altitude, and current weather patterns.

Higher elevations tend to transition into fall earlier, while the transformation occurs later at lower elevations. To optimize your journey, it's wise to consult local foliage forecasts and plan your trip to coincide with nature's peak performance. The splendor of the changing leaves can be witnessed across most of Colorado east of I-25 with the best spots at higher elevations.

For those fortunate enough to find themselves in Colorado during the fall season, I wholeheartedly recommend a mountain drive to experience the full glory of autumn's palette.

Whether you're an avid leaf peeper or simply someone who appreciates the grandeur of nature, the experience is sure to leave a lasting impression. So, join us in our annual tradition and discover the enchanting magic of Colorado's fall foliage for yourself.

# CHAPTER 26

# FORT COLLINS

## NATURAL BEACON SCULPTED BY TIME, ADMIRED BY ALL

As you approach **Fort Collins** *"Foco"*, the landscape unfolds with the iconic ***Horsetooth Mountain*** serving as a stunning backdrop. A mountain hill adorned with a white "A" stands proudly, a nod to the former *Aggie College football team*.

The mountain's silhouette, resembling a horse's tooth, is more than just a unique geological feature, it carries a legend. According to Native American lore, a giant's heart was once pierced by a desperate tribe's axe, which turned the soil red and petrified his bleeding heart into the massive, cracked rock we see today. This tragic transformation occurred when a man came and killed all the animals in the land that the giant was protecting. However, the name we now use came later from *Euro-Americans* who thought it resembled a horse's tooth.

The construction of ***Horsetooth Reservoir*** dams began in 1937, as a part of the larger Big Thompson Project. The town of Stout was abandoned by 1949 to make way for the reservoir, which was filled by 1951 and took five years to reach its full capacity.[1,2] At times when the water levels were low, the steeple of a submerged church would eerily emerge, and it became a popular spot for scuba divers to receive their certification.

However, remnants of Stout have since vanished, particularly after the reservoir was drained in the early 2000s for dam repairs. An additional layer of sand and gravel was laid down, forever altering the lakebed. Watching the once-vast lake nearly emptied was a poignant chapter of my childhood, as construction workers toiled to fortify the dams.

A Gateway to natural splendor. Today, with the reservoir's waters once again brimming, *Horsetooth Reservoir* stands as one of the most cherished landscapes in the Fort Collins area. It's a sanctuary for water enthusiasts and nature lovers alike, offering a serene setting for kayaking, boating, paddle boarding, and shoreline picnics. You can even rent pontoon boats with slides. The lake features several beaches right on the water, some of which offer campsites and day-use areas with barbecues. A brief drive from the heart of Fort Collins transports you to this oasis of outdoor recreation.

For adventurers and hikers, *Horsetooth Reservoir* provides two distinct trails that promise breathtaking views and an opportunity to immerse oneself in the tranquility of nature.

Both trails start at ***Horsetooth Mountain Trailhead***. One trail leads to the summit of the mountain, where you can stand atop the mountain peak with the famed "tooth" formation, while the other, ***Horsetooth Falls*** trail, is a more moderate 2.2-mile hike that rewards trekkers with the sights and sounds of a picturesque waterfall.

Whether you're in search of a challenging ascent or a peaceful walk to the falls, Horsetooth offers a perfect escape into Colorado's rugged beauty. Talk about a killer view at the top. I've also seen people rock climbing to the very top of the tooth. I love rappelling down the ropes; however, it's the climbing up part I have a problem with. Any of you who practice that sport are amazing, I applaud you.

*Fort Collins, Colorado*, is my stomping ground. My best friend from Costa Rica will be arriving soon, and she has just asked for our itinerary. Twenty-four hours is not much time; however, we plan to see the best parts. They've rented a car, which allows them to meet us at the **Cache La Poudre River**, right before you head up the canyon. About thirty minutes up the windy road, there are pull-offs for cars. This allows us to pull over and get the kids out to play in the river. Even though it's July, the water is cold, in my opinion, but the younger kids didn't seem to mind as they played in the river.

In less than an hour, I was able to show my surfer friends what it's like to live by a river, not an ocean. Dozens of kayakers, whitewater rafters, and tubers passed through the rapid river as we sat on rocks and caught up on the past year of being in different countries.

Even when I was a young child, my parents would caution me about how dangerous the Colorado rivers were. That didn't stop us from enjoying the amazing rapids; it just made us more cautious. Enter the river at your own risk because these fast waters can be extremely dangerous. Emergency rescue services are far away; if an emergency occurs, it's hard to get help, and the riverbeds can change quickly. Just in the first few months of 2023, river deaths in Colorado are up compared to previous years: 18 people have died, and three are still missing.[3] If you ask my children, three of them will never tube on this river again because we ended up in a bad situation one year when it started raining, and the river dam was around the next corner. Even the adults, who were strong swimmers, had trouble pulling the kids out of the water. Life vests and my kids being strong swimmers were the only things that saved us.

**Fun Fort Collins Fact**: After a fun-filled couple of hours playing in the water, our appetites led us to seek out dinner. As we meandered through the streets, we were walking in the footsteps of history.

It's a little-known fact that our very own Fort Collins, Colorado, specifically the area we were in, inspired the creation of ***Disneyland's***

***Main Street USA***. *Harper Goff*, a Fort Collins native like myself, grew up here and later shared his love for the town's quaint charm with *Walt Disney*.[4] Together, they transformed those small-town memories into a magical, nostalgic main street that would enchant visitors from around the globe.

Even though decades have passed, and much has changed, the essence of Old Town Fort Collins remains. Notably, the ***Old Linden Hotel*** still stands, its facade largely unchanged, serving as a tangible link to the past. While the names of the surrounding restaurants have varied over time, the area's charm is undiminished; you can still savor an eclectic mix of foods, much like in the old days, surrounded by the same historic beauty that once inspired a dream.

During the summer, the town might host festivals or concerts, parades, events during *CSU* homecoming, and even St. Patrick's Day celebrations complete with marching bands and floats. Be sure to enjoy a green beer at one of the local pubs. Or take in a football game at the new stadium.

## A Journey Through Colorado's University Towns

Colorado is renowned for its prestigious universities, with standouts like *Colorado State University (CSU)* in Fort Collins, University of *Northern Colorado (UNC)* in Greeley, *University of Colorado Boulder (CU)* in Boulder, and not to be overlooked, *Colorado Mesa University (CMU)* in Grand Junction on the western slope. Growing up in Fort Collins, I naturally rooted for CSU, with CU as their famed rival. These college towns offer the chance to catch exciting sports events and tour the campuses, all complemented by great food and lively coffee shops.

The most noticeable change upon returning home is that while these towns are still bustling with young adults and scholars, the nightlife isn't quite as vibrant as I remember. Back in the day, bars were packed until last call at 2 AM. While some weekends still recapture that energy, many students now seem to enjoy the atmosphere earlier in the evening, around 8 PM.

I was fortunate to catch the last football game of the season at CSU's stadium, checking an item off my bucket list. I hadn't been to a game since the new stadium was built on campus. I really miss the old *Hughes Stadium*, nestled right under the "A" in Fort Collins, with its nostalgic feel  and ample parking. This time, taking the bus wasn't too bad, though it added an extra hour to our day out.

Fort Collins offers art, historical, and world cultural museums, as well as parks for kids to play in and old-time candy stores—all within walking distance. Another cool way to see the city is by using bike share and scooters, which you can rent throughout the town to take advantage of the amazing bike paths.

## A Thanksgiving 5K in Colorado's Old Town Turkey Trot

Have you ever been tempted to join the ranks of 5K runners? Colorado, with its scenic landscapes, offers an array of races perfect for both eager beginners and seasoned pros. On a crisp Thanksgiving morning, I joyfully crossed the ***Turkey Trot*** off my bucket list. The 4-mile journey wove through the picturesque streets of Fort Collins' starting in Old Town, and with my starting spot towards the rear, it felt as though an extra mile had been added just for me.

The atmosphere was a delightful mix of friendly rivalry and camaraderie; runners had gathered well before the race, their excitement palpable in the air. Some were there to compete, while others, like myself, simply looked forward to the experience.

My aim was modest, my goal was to just finish. I had resolved to maintain a brisk walking pace while my friends were determined to do a progression run picking up speed at each mile marker. Despite my efforts over the months, Steve remained unmoved by the prospect of running—his running joke was that he'd only sprint if something was chasing him.

Participating in the *Turkey Trot* was an incredibly uplifting and supportive experience. It filled me with a sense of achievement comparable to the rush of completing a challenging endeavor. The crowd's cheers were as invigorating as the cool, fresh air, giving me the boost I needed to reach the finish line with a heart brimming with thanks and a stride fueled by resolve.

## A Pedal-Powered Celebration in Fort Collins
## Tour de Fat

*Tour de Fat* is not just a bike ride; it's a costumed celebration on wheels that has become a beloved tradition in Fort Collins. Having lived in the city all my life, I only joined the ride shortly before moving abroad. It turned out to be the last grand biking event I shared with my children, and it's an experience I eagerly anticipate revisiting.

The journey begins at City Park, where you merge with a vibrant crowd of cyclists and simply let the festive stream guide you through the streets of Fort Collins. The route culminates at **New Belgium Brewing**, where the atmosphere buzzes with live music and jovial gatherings. It's a day where fun knows no age limit, although the post-parade party is reserved for those 21 and older.

From college students to seasoned adults, parents pushing strollers, and individuals on skateboards or bikes of all kinds, everyone is there for a good time. However, it's worth noting that if throngs of people aren't your thing, *Tour de Fat* might be overwhelming. The streets become a sea of participants, and once you're swept up in the parade's flow, it can be a challenge to find your way out. But for those who revel in the collective energy of a crowd, *Tour de Fat* is an unforgettable celebration of community, cycling, and craft beer.

*Tip*

*Make sure to celebrate responsibly. Having both ride-sharing apps at your fingertips allows you to compare availability and rates, ensuring you have a reliable and convenient transportation option when you're ready to call it a day. By planning ahead, you can focus on enjoying the vibrant atmosphere and unique experiences of the adult drinks in Colorado without compromising your safety or that of others on the road.*

What are you interested in? There's a wide variety of tours available. Whether you're in the mood for something spooky or perhaps historical, there's plenty to choose from. Still on my bucket list is the **ghost tour** that delves into the underground world of Fort Collins. Alternatively, you could opt for a **brewery tou**r or simply soak up some caffeine at one of the local **coffee shops**.

### Holiday Magic

If you happen to visit during the winter season you will not be let down. Fort Collins boasts beautiful holiday lights. This year, I had the privilege of attending the lighting ceremony for the first time.

It was a delightful evening; the streets of Fort Collins became packed with people as the town flipped the switch to illuminate the holiday lights. There's nothing better to get you into the festive spirit than strolling through the quaint streets of Old Town and soaking in all the seasonal charm.

As you can see, Fort Collins, Colorado, is a year-round destination with so much to offer. No matter what you're searching for, this iconic town has something new around every corner.

CHAPTER 27

# FINAL THOUGHTS

## COLORADO THROUGH THE EYES OF A LOCAL

After sharing my Colorado experiences with you my five senses are on traveler's overload, and I'm loving every bit of it. I encourage you to stop and let your body embrace the moment. Your sights, smells, tastes, touch, and even the sounds of Colorado are incredible. My grandpa would always tell me to slow down in life; to do this, we need to *stop and smell the flowers*. I wish he were here today; I would tell him we also need to stop and smell the pine trees.

On the topic of smell, it sounds crazy, and I thought my sister-in-law was playing a trick on me during our first camping trip when she told me that, the trunks of the pine trees smelled like butterscotch. The Colorado woods have a beautiful smell of pine from the needles and pollen, but I had never put my nose to one and taken a deep breath of the bark of the tree. It's a smell she said she had missed since moving to Texas.

Now I know I got much the same look the day I snapped this picture. It's of my bestie after I convinced her to take a sniff of the tree. Over the last two decades, I have smelled pine trees over dozens of mountaintops and it's a smell I've missed dearly during extended stays outside the country.

The summits and mountaintops that greeted me home still leave me breathless and emotional. The defining beauty of Colorado is something that should be on every traveler's bucket list.

Steve and I have been incredibly fortunate to once again experience the awe-inspiring vistas from atop these mountain peaks. Our Colorado adventures have been filled with joyous moments, from lively game nights by the pool to relaxing in resort hot tubs, fishing in pristine waters, and embarking on scenic drives.

We've even had the pleasure of taking fall hikes with Grandpa and my sister-in-law, pausing to immerse ourselves in the scents and marvels of the Colorado landscape. Gathering around the outdoor fire pit for family dinners with our adult children has been a true highlight, creating precious memories that hold more value than the gold and green hues adorning the hills.

Savoring a nightcap to take in a gorgeous sunset as I let the day's worries go my thoughts are that I hope this book gives you a glimpse into the wonders of the Colorado and the gorgeous Rocky Mountains.

I enjoy a hot cup of coffee in the morning with Mr. Sun as we welcome the gorgeous sunrise from the road. Wanderlust and a road that could lead anywhere. I'm so full of gratitude to be able to experience it. The sights of Colorado have been etched in my soul, and the roads seem to be endless.

To my family and friends, we have to say goodbye again. Our flight has been booked and our luggage is packed, but this is not the end. I would love to travel more with you. So, make sure to stay tuned until we meet again, and safe travels. I hope that you have an amazing journey and discover what you are looking for in this great big world.

### *The End!*

# ABOUT THE AUTHOR
## NIKKI PAGE

As the co-founder of Viva Purpose, Inc., this remarkable woman has created writings that instruct, educate, and entertain. She is a seasoned writer and traveler. Delve into the literary world of *Nikki Page*, where each book is a journey of its own, brimming with insights, imagination, and the power to transform. Discover her collection of *#1 worldwide bestsellers* and see how her written words captivate and inspire readers around the globe.

# TRAVEL ART GALLERY

Embark on a visual journey around the world with our captivating ***Travel Art Gallery***.[1] Discover a curated collection of stunning photographs and artwork that showcase the beauty and diversity of global destinations, including works by ***Steve Page*** at ***Viva Purpose, Inc.***, ***Morgan Mosher*** and ***Taya Page*** *at* ***Peculiar Pieces***, and ***Jered Bridgeman*** at ***BridgemanPhotography***.[2,3,4 5]

The custom images featured in this book are available as high-quality prints, allowing you to bring a piece of your favorite destination into your own space.

# TRAVEL COLORADO DISCOUNTS, EXCURSIONS & LODGING ACCOMMODATIONS

Discover more of Colorado with exciting travel discounts. We have partnered with travel providers to help you find great deals on lodging, tours, and attractions. Our way of saying thank you. Unlock special offers and explore discounted accommodations, excursions, and more.

# ALSO BY NIKKI PAGE

Let's Travel the World: A Travel Guide and Tips for the 21st Century

Colorado Is Calling: Adventures in the Rocky Mountain State

The Essential RV, Camper, and Van Living Travel Guidebook: Embrace the Journey

Cut the Crap & Move to Costa Rica: A How-To Guide Based on These Gringos' Experience

Cut The Crap Kitchen: How-To Cook On A Budget In Costa Rica

228 Days Trapped in Paradise: The Diary of an Expat Chica in Costa Rica

# REFERENCES

## 2. DENVER INTERNATIONAL AIRPORT: DIA

1. *Denver International Airport (DIA):*
   https://www.flydenver.com/
2. *Forbes: Conspiracy New World Airport Commission:*
   https://www.forbes.com/sites/brittanyanas/2023/10/30/why-the-denver-airport-started-embracing-its-conspiracy-theories/?sh=d742dbb7b766

## 3. THE MILE HIGH CITY - DENVER

1. *Red Rocks Amphitheater:*
   https://www.redrocksonline.com/
2. *The Crawford Hotel:*
   https://www.thecrawfordhotel.com/
3. *Travel Colorado Discounts, Excursions & Lodging Accommodations:*
   https://vivapurpose.com/colorado-is-calling-your-ultimate-guide-to-the-centennial-state/travel-colorado-discounts-excursions-lodging-accommodations/
4. *Union Station:*
   https://www.denverunionstation.com/about/
5. *Denver Art Museum:*
   https://www.denverartmuseum.org/en
6. *River North Art District (RiNo):*
   https://rinoartdistrict.org/
7. *Denver Children's Museum:*
   https://www.mychildsmuseum.org/
8. *Clyfford Still Museum:*
   https://bellcotheatre.com/
9. *Clyfford Still Museum:*
   https://clyffordstillmuseum.org/
10. *History Colorado Center:*
    https://www.kirklandmuseum.org/#/
11. *Molly Brown House Museum:*
    https://mollybrown.org/
12. https://www.denvercenter.org/
13. *State Capitol:*
    https://capitol.colorado.gov/
14. **Colorado Convention Center:**
    https://bluebearstudios.com/
15. *The White City of the West* :
    https://history.denverlibrary.org/news/western-history/history-lakeside-amusement-park-photos
16. *Lakeside Amusement Park:*
    https://www.lakesideamusementpark.com/

17. *Casa Bonita:*
     https://www.casabonitadenver.com/
18. *Casa Bonita, historical landmark*
     https://www.denverpost.com/2015/03/20/casa-bonita-named-lakewood-historical-society-landmark/
19. *Casa Bonita:*
     https://www.casabonitadenver.com/

## 4. EASTERN PLAINS BACK IN TIME

1. *Kit Carson Country Carousel:*
     https://www.burlingtoncolo.com/190/Kit-Carson-County-Carousel
2. *Paint Mines Interpretive Park*
     https://communityservices.elpasoco.com/parks-and-recreation/paint-mines-interpretive-park/
3. **National Register of Historic Places Registration Form:**
     https://npgallery.nps.gov/GetAsset/d125cf34-2511-4864-aa38-e8077c65d730
4. *Picket Wire Canyonlands:*
     https://www.fs.usda.gov/recarea/psicc/recarea/?recid=77620
5. *La Junta Tarantula festival:*
     https://visitlajunta.net/la-junta-tarantula-fest/
6. *Koshare Museum*, *Largest Self-Supported Log Roof in the World:*
     https://visitlajunta.net/play/koshare-indian-museum/
7. *Koshare Dancers*:
     https://visitlajunta.net/koshare-dancers/

## 5. COLORADO SPRINGS

1. *Colorado Springs Municipal Airport (COS):*
     https://coloradosprings.gov/flycos
2. *United States Air Force Academy:*
     https://www.usafa.edu/visitors/
3. *Twenty-five Year Award* **from the American Institute of Architects:**
     https://www.aia.org/design-excellence/awards/twenty-five-year-award
4. *National Historic Landmark:*
     https://www.docomomo-us.org/register/united-states-air-force-academy-cadet-chapel
5. **Cheyenne Mountain Complex:**
     https://www.northcom.mil/CheyenneMountain/
6. **Cheyenne Mountain Complex:**
     https://en.wikipedia.org/wiki/Cheyenne_Mountain_Complex
7. **Olympic and Paralympic Training Center:**
     https://www.teamusa.com/visit
8. *Garden of the Gods:*
     https://gardenofgods.com/park-info/
9. *Garden of the Gods Free and Public Forever:*
     https://www.cspm.org/cos-150-story/garden-of-the-gods/
10. *Patsy's Candies:*
     https://patsyscandies.com/

11. *Cog Railway:*
    https://www.cograilway.com/
12. *Manitou Springs Incline*:
    https://manitousprings.org/where-to-play/manitou-incline/
13. *The North Pole Colorado:*
    https://northpolecolorado.com/
14. *The Race to the Clouds:*
    https://ppihc.org/race-to-the-clouds/
15. *Cave of the Winds:*
    https://caveofthewinds.com/cave-tours/
16. *Broadmoor Seven Falls:*
    https://www.sevenfalls.com/discover/hiking-trails
17. *The Broadmoor Resort*:
    https://www.denverpost.com/2021/02/23/the-broadmoor-forbes-5-star-hotel/
18. *George W. Bush hangover:*
    https://www.washingtonpost.com/wp-srv/politics/campaigns/wh2000/stories/bush072599.htm
19. *USA Today- Voted 5 Best Zoos:*
    https://www.cmzoo.org/news/archive/cheyenne-mountain-zoo-voted-5-best-zoo-in-north-america-by-usa-today-10best-readers-choice-awards/
20. *TripAdvisor World's Top Zoos:*
    https://www.usatoday.com/picture-gallery/travel/destinations/2015/07/14/tripadvisor-names-the-worlds-top-zoos/30149135/
21. *Royal Gorge Bridge:*
    https://royalgorgebridge.com/

## 6. THE AMERICAN SPIRIT BISHOP CASTLE

1. *Bishop Castle:*
    https://www.bishopcastle.org/about/
2. *Denver 7 News - Jim Bishop:*
    https://www.denver7.com/news/contact-denver7/denver7-gives/man-behind-legendary-bishop-castle-in-need-of-adaptive-wheelchair

## 7. DUNES OF WONDER

1. *The Great Sand Dunes National Park:*
    https://www.nps.gov/grsa/index.htm
2. *The Sand Dunes Recreation:*
    https://www.sanddunespool.com/about-us

## 8. MESA VERDE

1. *Mesa Verde National Park:*
    https://www.nps.gov/meve/index.htm

## 9. RED ROCKS AMPHITHEATER

1. **Red Rocks Amphitheater:**
   https://www.redrocksonline.com/

## 10. TEATIME & BOULDER ADVENTURES

1. *Boulder Canyon:*
   https://www.fs.usda.gov/recarea/arp/recarea/?recid=40354
2. *Eldorado Canyon State Park:*
   https://cpw.state.co.us/placestogo/parks/EldoradoCanyon
3. *Boulder Reservoir:*
   https://bouldercolorado.gov/locations/boulder-reservoir
4. *South Boulder Creek:*
   https://www.fs.usda.gov/recarea/arp/recarea/?recid=28344
5. *Celestial Seasonings*https://celestialseasonings.com/pages/tea-tour
6. *University of Colorado Boulder (CU):*
   https://www.colorado.edu/
7. *Colorado State University (CSU):*
   https://www.colostate.edu/
8. *Valmont Bike Park:*
   https://bouldercolorado.gov/locations/valmont-bike-park

## 12. FROM GOLD RUSH TO BLACKJACK RUSH

1. *Spirit Hound Distillers:*
   https://www.spirithounds.com/about-us
2. *Knotted Root Brewing Company:*
   https://www.knottedrootbrewing.com/home
3. **USA Today, top hotel spas in the nation:**
   https://monarch-casino.mandccommunications.com/the-votes-are-in-and-spa-monarch-is-honored-as-one-of-the-top-spas-in-america-by-usa-today-voters

## 13. NOT GOLD IN THEM HILLS, IT'S GREEN

1. *Annie's first US recreational cannabis shop:*
   https://mjbizdaily.com/first-recreational-cannabis-license-in-history-award-ed/https://mjbizdaily.com/first-recreational-cannabis-license-in-history-awarded/

## 14. TAKE IT ALL OFF

1. *Westbound & Down Brewing Company:*
   https://westboundanddown.com/
2. *Idaho Springs:*
   https://indianhotsprings.com/
3. *Glenwood Springs:*
   https://www.cogs.us/

## 15. COLORADO'S YEAR-ROUND ALPINE PLAYGROUND

1. ***Noble Buck Brewing Co:***
   https://www.thenoblebuck.com/
2. ***First Ever Gondola Vail:***
   https://discovervail.com/vail-stories-yellow-gondola/#:
3. **Strawberry Park Hot Springs:**
   https://strawberryhotsprings.com/
4. ***Nikola Tesla:***
   https://www.telluride.com/discover/blog/teslas-telluride-connection/

## 16. HOLLYWOOD BACKDROP

1. ***Film in Colorado:***
   https://www.filmincolorado.com/resources/filmography/
2. ***Filming locations Die Hard:***
   https://www.imdb.com/title/tt0099423/locations/

## 17. BUC-EE'S

1. ***Fox 31 KDVR Denver News:***
   https://buc-ees.com/
2. ***Buc-ee's 116-pump gas station:***
   https://www.denverpost.com/2023/12/08/colorado-bucees-store-johnston-convenience/

## 18. NATURES UNEXPECTED NIGHTLIGHT

1. Jered at ***BridgemanPhotography***
   https://fineartamerica.com/profiles/jered-bridgeman

## 19. LOVELAND COLORADO

1. ***Loveland, Colorado valentine re-mailing program.***
   https://loveland.org/programs/valentine-re-mailing-program/

## 20. THE BIG THOMPSON RIVER

1. ***USGS:***
   https://www.usgs.gov/news/state-news-release/big-thompson-canyon-floods-1976-and-2013-tale-two-deadly-and-destructive

## 21. ESTES PARK

1. ***Rocky Mountain National Parks Visitor Centers:***
   https://www.nps.gov/romo/planyourvisit/visitorcenters.htm

## 22. STANDING ON TOP OF THE WORLD

1. *Rocky Mountain National Park:*
   https://www.nps.gov/romo/index.htm
2. *Longs Peak:*
   https://www.nps.gov/romo/planyourvisit/longspeak.htm

## 23. LAKES - CAMPING - HUNTING & FISHING

1. *Lory State Park:*
   https://cpw.state.co.us/placestogo/parks/Lory
   *Roosevelt National Forest:*
   https://www.fs.usda.gov/arp
   *Steamboat Springs*
   https://cpw.state.co.us/placestogo/parks/SteamboatLake
2. *Lake Granby:*
   https://www.recreation.gov/camping/gateways/68
3. *Grand Lake:*
   https://www.townofgrandlake.com/
4. **Red Feather Lakes:**
   https://www.fs.usda.gov/recarea/arp/recarea/?recid=77700
5. **Roosevelt National Forest:**
   https://www.fs.usda.gov/arp
6. *Dowdy:*
   https://www.fs.usda.gov/recarea/arp/recarea/?recid=36653
7. *Bellaire Lake Campground:*
   https://www.recreation.gov/camping/campgrounds/233137
8. *Drala Mountain Center:*
   http://www.shambhalamountain.org/

## 24. MAKE YOUR TASTE BUDS DANCE

1. *Rocky Ford Watermelons:*
   http://rockyfordmelons.com/history/watermelon-day-history/

## 26. FORT COLLINS

1. *Horsetooth Reservoir:*
   https://www.larimer.gov/naturalresources/parks/horsetooth-reservoir
2. *Horsetooth Reservoir History:*
   https://cpw.state.co.us/placestogo/parks/Lory/Pages/History.aspx
3. **2023 Cache La Poudre River Deaths:**
   https://www.summitdaily.com/news/river-deaths-in-2023-are-on-the-rise-in-colorado/
4. **Harper Goff, Fort Collins Main Street:**
   https://history.fcgov.com/legends/disney

## TRAVEL ART GALLERY

1. ***Travel Art Gallery:***
   https://vivapurpose.com/travel-art-gallery/
2. ***Viva Purpose, Inc.***
   https://vivapurpose.com/
   ***CEO Steve Page:***
   vivapurpose.com/book-keynote-speaker-ceo-1-bestselling-author-steve-page
3. ***Morgan Mosher: Peculiar Pieces***
   https://peculiarpieces.art/morgan
   https://peculiarpieces.art/
4. ***Taya Page: Peculiar Pieces:***
   https://peculiarpieces.art/taya
   https://peculiarpieces.art/
5. ***Jered at BridgemanPhotography:***
   https://fineartamerica.com/profiles/jered-bridgeman

www.ingramcontent.com/pod-product-compliance
Lightning Source LLC
Chambersburg PA
CBHW040854120626
46551CB00001B/12